PARIS OBSERVED

Translated from the French
by Patrick Greene

Bracken Books
LONDON

CONTENTS

Published 1986 by Bracken Books, a division of Bestseller Publications Limited,
Princess House, 50 Eastcastle Street, London W1, England.

First published 1980 by Hachette.
This edition, Copyright © Bracken Books 1986

ISBN 1 85170 054 4

Design by Jean-Louis Germain. Printed in Italy by Milanostampa - Farigliano (Cuneo)

Every big city has its own unique charm, and Paris is no exception. Yet it is so many-sided a place that few people can claim to know it thoroughly, let alone try to define its spell. The city's grey streets and formal vistas seem to reveal their secrets quickly and generously to the newcomer, but such first impressions are... not so much misleading as incomplete. For Paris is more than the sum of its historic buildings, its museums, and its vast range of entertainment, and those who want to know it well must penetrate beneath its outer shell and try to understand what is perhaps its most special feature—the character of the people who live in it.

Relatively few of the people who live in Paris have deep family roots in the city; Parisians today come from every corner of the planet. But one thing they all have in common, and that is a certain attitude of mind. Blasé and tolerant, the Parisian contemplates life with a polite detachment which has more to do with courtesy than indifference to his fellow men.

It is possible to live in Paris for years without getting to know your neighbour who lives on the same landing, and yet within a matter of days you may be on friendly terms with the tobacconist who sells you your cigarettes or the waiter of a restaurant where you have eaten more than once. The visitor to Paris does not feel invisible, as he does in New York, nor the object of a welcome, as he does in Venice. Paris is a city where people can behave just as they wish, and this goes some way to explaining why the atmosphere of the city varies from quarter to quarter. One part of the city may be as quiet and secluded as a provincial town; another may hum with curiosity about anything and everything—and Paris is equipped to satisfy the appetite of the most insatiably curious. Paris is a mosaic of small communities, and each visitor forms an impression of it which reflects his own tastes and interests. But one thing everyone is bound to discover in Paris—a respect for nonconformity and freedom of spirit.

1
THE HEART OF PARIS: THE ISLANDS

Notre-Dame seen from the quays

Paris owes its existence to the Seine just as much as Ancient Egypt owed its existence to the Nile: the earliest settlement was on the island in the heart of the city called the Ile de la Cité. Today, 2,000 years later, Paris is a conurbation of more than 8 million people. It is a city in which each district has somehow managed to resist the onset of uniformity and keep its own distinct character, for although building has gradually eaten away at the green spaces which once lay between them, Paris is still very much a collection of villages, as it was centuries ago. It is, too, a place where visible reminders of history are abundant, and the visitor who strolls through Paris travels through time as well as space.

The ages have left their mark on **the Ile de la Cité and the Ile Saint-Louis**, whose rich fabric of history exercises a potent fascination on sightseers and artists alike. For on the quays nearby there is always at least one artist striving to put onto canvas his own version of **Notre-Dame's** silhouette, which has for eight centuries been reflected in the waters of the Seine. Paris grew in a spiral around the primitive settlement on the Ile de la Cité, which was used as a base by the boatmen who controlled the river traffic. After conquering the Gauls, Julius Caesar turned the village known to him as "Lutetia Parisiorum" into a Roman town. Two wooden bridges were built, linking the island to the river banks where the Rue Saint-Jacques is today. Incidentally, excavations of bones have shown that Rue Saint-Jacques follows the line of an ancient track taken by mammoths migrating to the South. Paris's first public buildings date from the Roman period: the Roman governor's villa stood on what in the Middle Ages became the site of the palace of the Capetian dynasty of French Kings, and a temple was built where the cathedral of Notre-Dame now stands.

Words set in heavy type refer to photographs on the same or the opposite page.

The Ile Saint-Louis and the Ile de la Cité

Apse and spire of Notre-Dame

Ironwork on the main door of Notre-Dame

The graceful lines of the slender **apse of Notre-Dame**, soaring above the broad fourteenth-century flying buttresses, inspired the poet Charles Péguy to compare the Ile de la Cité to a ship moored to the banks of the river. This image is so deeply inscribed in Paris history that its symbolism forms part of the city's coat of arms. Notre-Dame is one of several great cathedrals built in the royal cities of France during the 13th century. Though less complete than Chartres, less rich than Rheims, and less bold than Beauvais, it is a remarkable example of early Gothic architecture. Nevertheless, the powerfully marked horizontal lines on **the main façade** are still Romanesque. The cathedral's proportions would have been lightened if spires had been added to the 200-foot-high towers. As it is, Notre-Dame's single spire is a nineteenth-century reconstruction of the original by Viollet-le-Duc, the architect who restored the cathedral. Nowadays Viollet-le-Duc's audacity as a restorer has ceased to astonish, and whatever one's views about his

methods, we should remember that without him Notre-Dame would not have survived. The name of the original architect is unknown, but we do know that his plans were followed by the various master builders who worked on the cathedral during the 200 years after its foundation in 1163 by Maurice de Sully, bishop of Paris. The founder of Notre-Dame can still be seen on the south portal of the west façade, in prayer before the enthroned figure of the Virgin, who is depicted with an austerity that is entirely Romanesque as she watches over the entrance to the church dedicated to her. This tympanum is one of the few ancient pieces of stone carving in Notre-Dame which survived the Revolution, for most of the ornamental details and monumental carvings we can see today have been extensively and somewhat ponderously restored by Viollet-le-Duc. Nevertheless, some authentic pieces can still be seen, including the reliefs on the lower part of the main façade, the stained glass of the great rose windows, and the statue of the Virgin on the north portal. **The ironwork and hinges on the main door** show little animals at play among leafy scrolls; their workmanship is so exquisite that Parisians traditionally believed them to be the work of the devil himself.

Many great moments in French history have been celebrated in Notre-Dame, including royal marriages and baptisms, and the Te Deums sung in honour of great national victories—the most recent of these being held to celebrate the liberation of Paris on August 26, 1944. When the Kings of France made their solemn entry into the capital, they always went to Notre-Dame to pay their respects to the Virgin Mary. To celebrate the event, the sellers of caged birds, who already had shops in the area, on the nearby Pont au Change, would release hundreds of their winged captives. The cathedral has also played a part in French literary history: it was in the choir of Notre-Dame that the great French religious poet and man of letters Paul Claudel was converted to Christianity on Christmas Day 1886, while listening to the Magnificat being sung during Vespers. He recorded the exact spot where his conversion took place—near to the second pillar in front of the door of the sacristy. But the most remarkable event to take place in Notre-Dame was the coronation of Napoleon as Emperor on December 2, 1804. Napoleon did not want to follow the tradition whereby French rulers were crowned in Rheims cathedral, and decided to send for Pius VII to crown him in Paris.

Paris is unique in the annals of urban history in that the city developed along the two banks of its river simultaneously. In the Middle Ages, the settlement on the north bank—known at first as "Beyond the great

bridge," and later simply as "the city"—was a business and trading centre (it occupied roughly the site of Les Halles, where Paris's central food markets were situated until recently); the south bank, known at first as "Beyond the little bridge," and later as the university, was given over to intellectual activity.

During the Middle Ages, four wooden footbridges joined the Ile de la Cité to the settlements across the river. These medieval bridges were lined with houses which were not systematically demolished until the 18th century. The first stone bridge built without houses to link the two banks of the river directly dates from the end of the 16th century, when it was such a novelty that the Parisians called it simply "the new bridge"—the **Pont-Neuf**—as they still do. Its two spans rest on what was at the time a small island downstream from the Ile de la Cité. The foundation stone of the Pont-Neuf was laid in 1578 by Henri III, and Henri IV, who opened it in 1606, filled in the narrow creek which separated the bridge from the royal palace on the Ile de la Cité. A triangular square was laid out on the reclaimed land. The houses on it, like those in Place Royale, which was then being built in the Marais district, are of pink brick trimmed with stone, with steeply sloping slate roofs. Magistrates and judges lived on the square, which was named Place Dauphine in honour of the Dauphin, the heir to the throne, who was at that time the future Louis XIII. One side of the square was destroyed in the 19th century, but **two lovely houses** on Place du Pont-Neuf still look out on to the statue of Henri IV,

The Pont-Neuf and the Ile de la Cité

Houses on Place du Pont-Neuf; between them, the narrow entrance into Place Dauphine

The Pont-Neuf and the equestrian statue of Henri IV

the man who ordered them to be built. Henri IV's statue is exactly where it should be, in the heart of the city which owes him so much. In the 17th century it was the only equestrian statue in Paris, so that people would often arrange to meet "under the horse."

The original statue was knocked from its pedestal and destroyed during the Revolution. After the restoration of the monarchy, the bronze effigy of Napoleon on the Vendôme column came in for the same treatment: its bronze was melted down and used for the present statue on the Pont-Neuf. During the 17th century the **Pont-Neuf** and the area nearby became to Paris what the forum had been to Rome. It was a hive of colourful activity—dentists, pedlars, animal trainers and travelling entertainers of all kinds set up their booths there. Beneath the statue, the garden of the Vert Galant, which also takes its name from the gallant King Henri IV, was once the haunt of tramps. Today hippies and lovers

The Pont des Arts seen from the prow of the Ile de la Cité, with the Pont du Carrousel beyond

sit beneath the branches of the huge weeping willow on the island's sharp prow, and gaze towards the **Pont des Arts**, a footbridge built in 1803 which is still for pedestrian use only. This is one of the earliest examples of an iron structure in Paris. Napoleon I, who ordered the experimental iron bridge to be built, thought little of the result. Other people were less disappointed. A contemporary journalist wrote that the bridge was a place where one could always be sure "of meeting the best people on a fine summer evening," and among its attractions were the stalls of a florist and an ice vendor.

The clock set into the Tour de l'Horloge

The palace used for centuries by the Capetian dynasty of Kings of France which once stood on the Ile de la Cité was rebuilt several times before it was finally burned down in 1871. In other words, only the sturdiest of its buildings have survived the ravages of time. The part of the palace known as **the Conciergerie**, which looks out over the Seine on the north bank of the island has many ancient features. It is the only surviving part of the fortified enceinte which surrounded the Palace when the Kings lived in it. Three round towers are set into the wall of the Conciergerie, while the square tower on the north corner of the building contains Paris's first public **clock**, which was erected on this site on the orders of King Charles V in 1334. The present decoration of the clock dates from the time of Henri III, who commissioned the figures of Law and Justice which stand on each side of the clock face from the sculptor Germain Pilon. The arms of France and Poland are set above the clock as a reminder that Henri III had

been King of Poland before he succeeded to the French throne.

At the end of the 14th century, French Kings ceased to live in the Palace, which was taken over by the Supreme Court of Justice, the Parlement. The Conciergerie itself became a prison. The Supreme Court sat in an upper room, in the former royal apartments, and prisoners due to be tried were imprisoned in ground floor rooms until they were needed in court. However, criminal, as opposed to civil offences, were rarely tried in the Palace at this period; most criminals were tried in the Châtelet fortress on the other side of the Seine. During the Revolution, the tribunal which organized the Reign of Terror to purge the Revolution of its enemies sat in the Great Chamber formerly used by the Supreme Court, and condemned prisoners spent several days in the Conciergerie before going to the guillotine. Queen Marie-Antoinette, the Conciergerie's most famous prisoner, spent six months there, but this was exceptionally long. There are few direct reminders

of Marie-Antoinette's imprisonment today, for after the Revolution had run its course and the monarchy had been restored, her cell was transformed into a chapel. The sinister drama of the Reign of Terror can be felt more vividly in the prison corridors, which have not changed; in the small recreation yard (where the fountain in which the women washed their clothes can still be seen); and in the chapel, where the ill-fated revolutionary faction known to history as the Girondins spent their last night on earth before they were guillotined in 1793. The atmosphere of the Conciergerie is still gloomy; even today it is a temporary prison, and behind its barred windows are prisoners awaiting trial in the law courts of the Palais de Justice, of which the Conciergerie building forms part. An aura of tragedy also pervades the corridor along which condemned prisoners took their final walk, but today the room through which they passed on their way to the forecourt, and the tumbrils which took them to execution, is a lawyers' buffet.

The Conciergerie

Another building which dates from the time when the Palace was a royal residence still stands in the gloomy courtyard of the Palais de Justice, like some imprisoned princess trapped in sombre surroundings. The **Sainte-Chapelle** is one of the masterpieces of French architecture, and a monument to the piety of Louis IX—St. Louis —who built it. He decided to build the Sainte-Chapelle to house the relics of the Passion, including a piece of the True Cross, which he had bought from the Emperor of Constantinople. Built between 1245 and 1248, the Sainte-Chapelle is, like the Parthenon, the sum of the efforts of the finest craftsmen and artists of its age. The master builder is thought by some to have been Pierre de Montreuil, who built the south transept of Notre-Dame. Like most royal chapels, the Sainte-Chapelle has two stories: one at ground level for the Palace servants, and a **high chapel** on the same story as the King's apartments. In the latter the principles of Gothic construction were taken to their ultimate conclusion. The weight of the vaulting is carried by the pointed arches onto pillars which are supported by the massive masonry of the buttresses outside. Because the walls play no part in supporting the vaulting, it was possible for huge windows to be cut into them, creating the effect of an enormous reliquary with luminous sides. The original polychrome work in the chapel has been restored with more zeal than finesse, but in the warm, shimmering atmosphere it does not attract much attention to itself. The stained glass has been more skilfully restored, and in the first window on the right we can still follow the story of how the sacred relics were brought back from Venice by St. Louis's emissaries. The King himself went as far as Villeneuve-sur-Yonne, south of Paris, to take charge of them, and carried them part of the way back, walking barefoot. The Sainte-Chapelle today is the only church in Paris where it is possible to imagine exactly what a medieval building almost entirely covered with stained glass must have looked like.

Apart from some of the statues of the Apostles at the foot of the pillars, the original statuary has not survived. The delicacy of the stone carving is remarkable: the capitals are not only decorated in the usual manner with acanthus leaves, but with eglantine flowers, which some think may have been the trademark of Pierre de Montreuil. The rose-window of the façade, with its turbulent lines, dates from the end of the 15th century and contrasts sharply with the classical rigour of the rest of the chapel.

The King's private chapel was used for family ceremonies, royal marriages, and the coronation of the Queen. The Kings of France had one special link with

The Sainte-Chapelle

The high chapel in the Sainte-Chapelle

The Seine: mooring on the Quai du Louvre

the Sainte-Chapelle; each of them always carried with him the key to the shrine containing the sacred relics. The shrine was desecrated during the Revolution, like so many religious monuments, and restored in the 19th century. Those relics which have survived are preserved in Notre-Dame.

In the distant past, the public life of Paris was concentrated on and around the Ile de la Cité. Today the Palace is still occupied by law courts, as it was after the royal family ceased to live in it, while Paris police headquarters is in the building on the Quai des Orfèvres which has entered the popular imagination through Georges Simenon's Maigret novels. Across the Pont au Change on the Right Bank of the Seine, is the site of the Châtelet. Once a prison and a law court, today it is famous only for the Theatre of the Châtelet, which specializes in lavishly staged musicals. Not far away, on the same side of the river, rises the massive silhouette of Paris's city hall, the Hôtel de Ville, which was burned down in 1871 and then rebuilt in Renaissance style to be as faithful an imitation as possible of the building it replaced. Inside the Hôtel de Ville, the decoration reflects all that is most wearisome in official art. And yet the city authorities wanted, in their own words, "it to reflect in the very widest and most comprehensive sense the artistic movement of our age, without any restrictions and accepting all the consequences..." There can be no doubt that the city fathers were badly informed, for the work of the honest journeymen who decorated the Hôtel de Ville has not stood the test of time, and the visitor looks in vain for the names of Manet, Renoir, Dufy, Vuillard, and other fine artists of the period.

The square in front of the Hôtel de Ville no longer has any atmosphere, and it takes an enormous effort to imagine what it looked like in the days when it was called Place de Grève and was the place where public executions were held. These executions attracted immense crowds, especially when the victim was well known, like Ravaillac, the man who killed Henri IV in 1610, and the Marquise de Brinvilliers, a notorious seventeenth-century poisoner, who was beheaded and burned on Place de Grève. The first guillotine was erected on the square on August 25, 1792, and the last execution to be held there took place in 1832.

The Seine is still a great artery of navigation, as it was in the Middle Ages, although Paris is no longer France's biggest port in terms of tonnage. However, it is relatively cheap to transport heavy cargoes by water, and there are still plenty of **barges** on the river. Some of them have been converted into houseboats and are permanently moored near the Pont des Arts and the Pont-Royal. Another familiar sight on the banks of the Seine is

Barges on the Seine

The Flower Market on the Ile de la Cité

The Bird Market, Quai de la Mégisserie

the fishermen, who often seem more interested in the act of fishing for its own sake than in actually catching fish. For the Seine is not the river it was in the late 16th century, when the future King Henri IV, then living in the Louvre and afraid of being poisoned, came down to the river each morning with a jug to draw his own personal supply of drinking water. Today the water of the Seine is hardly pure enough for edible fish to survive in it and provide the fishermen with sport.

On the Ile de la Cité, opposite the Hôtel de Ville, is the **Flower Market**. The stalls of bush and plant sellers stretch along the quay, while the premises of the cut flower sellers are in the covered market nearby. All Paris florists, from the owners of the luxurious and expensive shops in the city centre to the traders who set up their stalls here and there in the streets, buy their flowers from wholesalers. They are required by law to buy a license, except on Palm Sunday and May 1, when anyone is free to sell the fronds of boxwood and the lilies of the valley which are traditionally bought by the French on these days. On Sundays, the site of the Flower Market is taken over by the **Bird Market**, which is held during the week on the Quai de la Mégisserie, on the other side of the Seine.

In the past the Seine was dotted with a string of small islands. Some of them disappeared altogether, others have been joined up to the river bank. The **Ile Saint-Louis**, upstream from the Ile de la Cité, was formed from two of these islands, Notre-Dame Island and the Isle of Cows. The latter, as its name suggests, was originally meadow land. The Isle of Cows was owned by the canons of the cathedral, who were opposed to its being used for building. One of the things they were afraid of was that if houses were built on the island, smoke from the kitchen fires would pollute the pure air of the Ile de la Cité. When they finally relented, in 1614, it was on condition that the two islands should never be joined. The building concession went to an entrepreneur named Marie, whose name is commemorated in the Pont-Marie, the bridge which connects the Ile Saint-Louis to the Right Bank of the Seine.

By the middle of the 17th century almost all the land had been built on, and the French aristocracy crossed the Seine from the nearby Marais district where they lived, to settle in the magnificent houses which now stood on the quays of the Ile Saint-Louis. The **Hôtel Chenizot**, a superb example of the rococo style, with its wrought-iron balconies supported by chimeras, is one of the island's few eighteenth-century buildings.

One of the most famous buildings on the island to have survived is the Hôtel Lauzun, which belongs to the city of Paris and is used for entertaining important guests of the city. The gallant and amorous Duke of Lauzun, who married Louis XIV's cousin, the "Grande Mademoiselle," lived for three years in the house which bears his name. It can still be visited. At the eastern end of the island, the Hôtel Lambert de Thorigny has been magnificently restored by its present occupant, who holds receptions worthy of the 17th century itself, but rarely allows it to be visited.

The Ile Saint-Louis is one of the most delightful as well as one of the most sought-after residential districts of Paris. Traffic is not allowed on the streets in the heart of the island, except for those who have the good fortune to live there, and the Ile Saint-Louis suffers less than the Ile de la Cité from the tourist invasion. The sunny quays are the most agreeable parts of the island to modern taste, but the finest houses are on the northern side, where poets like Théophile Gautier and Charles Baudelaire lived in the 19th century. The best time to visit the Ile Saint-Louis is at the end of the day, when the sun is setting behind Notre-Dame. Here on the island the imaginative visitor cannot help but feel the magic of Paris and the charm which keeps Parisians faithful to their city in spite of the intrusive noise and bustle of the modern world.

The Ile Saint-Louis: the Pont-Marie

The Ile Saint-Louis: the Hôtel Chenizot, 51 Rue Saint-Louis-en-l'Ile

2

SAINT-GERMAIN-DES-PRÉS

The Brasserie Lipp, Boulevard Saint-Germain

Ever since the Middle Ages, Paris intellectual life has been centred on the Left Bank of the Seine, while the Right Bank has traditionally been the business area. On the Left Bank, the Latin Quarter earned its name because Latin was the common language of the scholars from all over Europe who gathered there in medieval times. Today it is still the focus of Paris student life that it was then. But one of the liveliest districts on the Left Bank today is **Saint-Germain-des-Prés**, once a settlement which lay outside the boundaries of the medieval city.

The **abbey church of Saint-Germain-des-Prés** was founded in 558 A.D. by King Childebert, the son of Clovis, the first Christian King of Gaul, on a site which then lay in open country. It takes its name from Germain, a sixth-century bishop of Paris whose tomb was preserved in the abbey until the Revolution. When Paris became a walled city, the abbey stood in the "faubourg," or suburb, outside the city walls. People—and there were many of them—who wanted to escape from royal jurisdiction by living outside the city, began to settle around the abbey, and by the 17th century Saint-Germain-des-Prés had become a fashionable district. Tourist guidebooks of the period recommend visitors to Paris who want to have a good time to find lodgings there. Today, Saint-Germain-des-Prés still has something of a village atmosphere, in spite of an influx of people from all over the world. The newcomers are given a polite welcome by the local people, but although they are accepted, Saint-Germain-des-Prés is like any other village in that it takes a long time to feel really at home and to be a part of the community.

The beautiful church of Saint-Germain-des-Prés is one of the oldest in Paris. Only one of its original three towers has survived, although the

The abbey church of Saint-Germain-des-Prés reflected in the window of an antique shop on Rue Bonaparte

The Café de Flore

back to the time during the war when Jean-Paul Sartre preferred to write there rather than stay in his unheated apartment nearby. Today these places attract a wider cross-section of the public, if only because many people are drawn to Saint-Germain-des-Prés by the prospect of seeing Paris celebrities at close quarters. There are other attractions too: the restaurants and some of the shops stay open late and the window displays are always brightly lit and attractive.

The literary café is not a new phenomenon in Paris. In fact it has a long pedigree stretching back to the

The Procope Restaurant, Rue de l'Ancienne-Comédie

bases of the other two can still be seen beside the transept. Only a few stones have survived of the chapel built outside the church by Pierre de Montreuil, the thirteenth-century mason who may also have built the Sainte-Chapelle. These remains, in the garden on the corner of the square, make a curious contrast with a Picasso bust which stands there in memory of the poet Guillaume Apollinaire. Another relic of the original abbey buildings came to light not long ago, when part of the Gothic window of the monks' refectory was discovered in the wall of number 12 Rue de l'Abbaye, which runs parallel to the church. The choir, which was completed in 1163, is a good example of early Gothic. In the 19th century, the Romanesque nave was decorated with a series of paintings which fit uncomfortably into their surroundings.

However, most of the visitors to Saint-Germain-des-Prés do not come primarily to see the church, fine though it is. They come to sit in the quarter's famous cafés and restaurants, places like the Brasserie Lipp and the **Café de Flore**, on Boulevard Saint-Germain, and the **Deux Magots**, whose terrace opposite the church is the pleasantest in the area. Each of these old-established cafés and restaurants has a reputation for a certain kind of clientele: actors and politicians traditionally eat at Lipp; artists and men of letters go to the Deux Magots; while stars and people in the public eye tend to favour the Café de Flore, whose fame goes

end of the 17th century, when the city's only theatre was in a street then called Rue des Fossés-Saint-Germain, and since renamed Rue de l'Ancienne-Comédie. (The theatre's façade can still be seen at number 14.) Inside, the theatre was so mean and shabby that the actors and playwrights formed the habit of meeting in nearby cafés. Their favourite was the first café in Paris, an establishment owned by an astute Italian, Signor Procopio. His venture was a lasting success. The **Café Procope** has been open continuously since 1689, and still stands on its original site. The tradition of fine and ceremonious language which began with its first customers seems to have survived, for not long ago a waitress at the Procope was heard to issue the following majestic rebuke to a customer who had dared to make a slangy remark: "Sir, these words of yours do not seem to me to be worthy of the Procope." Before the Revolution, the only Paris streets to be lit at night were those leading to the theatre, and even today the streets around Rue de l'Ancienne-Comédie are some of the brightest in Paris:

Waiters outside the Café des Deux Magots

Students in the Latin Quarter

Place Furstenberg

Saint-Germain-des-Prés is one of the few places left in Paris where waiters still wear their traditional uniform—the waistcoat with a different pocket for each kind of coin, and the long white apron. At the Brasserie Lipp other traditions have been preserved: its turn of the century decor, its menu which never changes, and its ultra-Parisian clientele. There is almost always at least one well-known actor or politician to be found at Lipp and the staff have had an excellent training in the art of protecting their customers from public curiosity. Autograph hunters and star-spotters find it hard to get close to their idols at Lipp, and customers who show a persistent and indecorous curiosity are politely but firmly shown the door.

Most of the relatively few **students** to be seen around Saint-Germain-des-Prés are from the nearby École des Beaux-Arts, the Paris school of architecture and the graphic arts. Unfortunately it is not easy to get permission to visit the school's historically interesting buildings in Rue Bonaparte, on a site where the palace of Queen Margot, the wife of Henri IV, once stood.

The Beaux-Arts students bring plenty of colour and excitement into the life of the quarter. They organize fancy-dress processions and have their own **brass band**, which occasionally gives an improvised jazz concert on the terrace of the Deux Magots during fine weather. Unlike the other amateur musicians who perform on the pavements nearby, they do not pass the hat around afterwards.

Near to the church of Saint-Germain is **Place Furstenberg**, once the site of the abbey's stable yard. Opposite the entrance to the Place is the brick and stone building where the abbots lived. Place Furstenberg itself, where the painter Eugène Delacroix spent the last

The Beaux-Arts brass band

six years of his life, has a quiet, old-fashioned charm. It should be seen at dusk, when the lamps have been lit. The house where Delacroix lived is now a museum, and each year the Society of Friends of the painter holds an exhibition in his apartment and studio, which, contrary to usual practice, catches the midday sun. Admirers of Delacroix's work can also visit the church of Saint-Sulpice, not far away, where one of the chapels contains the magnificent frescoes of *Heliodorus chased from the Temple* and *Jacob's Fight with the Angel*, which he painted between 1855 and 1861. These pictures are Delacroix's spiritual testament, and it is entirely fitting that they should be in a part of Paris which has always attracted painters. The Le Nain brothers worked here in the 17th century, Chardin in the

"Philomène": 15 Rue Vavin

18th, and Ingres and Delacroix himself in the 19th. A later inhabitant of the district was Picasso, who painted *Guernica* in a studio in Rue des Grands-Augustins where the previous tenant had been the distinguished French actor-manager Jean-Louis Barrault.

Antique-dealing, publishing and bookselling are the traditional business activities of the Saint-Germain-des-Prés area, and around Saint-Sulpice there are a number of shops specializing in religious art. **Art galleries** dealing in avant-garde painting are another familiar part of the Saint-Germain scene; their traditional area is around the École des Beaux-Arts, but the newer ones are further away, on the fringe of the quarter. But the biggest change in this established pattern of trade came when the **fashion** business arrived in Saint-Germain. When the ready-to-wear boom began, the young lions of the industry looked around Paris for sites for new shops. There was nothing in the prestige Right Bank shopping area on and around the Faubourg Saint-Honoré, and so they came to Saint-Germain-des-Prés instead. Today the quarter is dotted with fashion shops with eye-catching window displays of clothes aimed at the youth market, and the streets are full of young people wearing their latest buys. Spend half an hour drinking an aperitif on a café terrace on Place Saint-Germain-des-Prés, and you will see more of the latest fashions than if you sit for a whole evening in other, staider parts of town.

Previously entrenched in the 8th Arrondissement on the Right Bank, some haute couture houses have followed the example of ready-to-wear and opened shops in the 6th. The most avant-garde of the grands couturiers, **Paco Rabanne**, has set up shop in one of the centres of the new Saint-Germain fashion district, Rue du Cherche-Midi. Originally trained as an architect, he is trying to revolutionize fashion by using materials like metal, celluloid and artificial furs.

The antique dealers of Saint-Germain-des-Prés are also trying to keep abreast of changes in public taste. Specialists in medieval and nineteenth-century objects have joined the hard core of dealers in eighteenth-century objects, and even kitsch, the ultimate refinement of bad taste, has arrived. Contemporary design shops have also opened up, so that Saint-Germain today can offer the whole range of styles and possibilities in decoration.

A Vasarely exhibition at the Denise René gallery, Boulevard Saint-Germain

Paco Rabanne, Rue du Cherche-Midi

La Gaminerie

The Absidiole café-theatre, 5 Rue Frédéric-Sauton

This kind of business is almost seasonal; it is, to say the least, dependent on the vagaries of fashion. And yet there is a strong thread of continuity running through life in Saint-Germain. Many people whose families have lived in the quarter for generations still buy from the children of the tradesmen their parents knew and trusted. For them life in Saint-Germain goes on independently of changing fashions.

Show business came relatively late to Saint-Germain-des-Prés. Before 1945 there were few theatres or cabarets. In fact there was only the uncomfortable Vieux-Colombier theatre, where a gifted actor and director named Jacques Copeau tried, in his own words, to create a theatre "free from the humiliating stupidity of the boulevard theatre." Copeau was helped by close friends from the theatre and literary worlds. Publisher Gaston Gallimard lent him capital; novelist Jules Romains rehearsed the actors; other writers and poets ran the cloakroom, checked the tickets and prompted the actors. Among the members of Copeau's original troupe were two of France's greatest men of the theatre this century, Louis Jouvet and Charles Dullin. In 1944, during the German occupation, the first performance of Jean-Paul Sartre's play *Huis Clos* took place at the Vieux-Colombier.

After the war there were no theatres available for the avant-garde cabaret shows which sprouted like mushrooms at that time. And so—like mushrooms—they flourished in cellars instead. The most famous of these cellars was the Rose Rouge in Rue de Rennes. It has long since closed its doors, but in the immediate postwar years it was a hotbed of talent, and many of the performers who appeared there went on to make their names elsewhere. They included future international stars like Juliette Gréco, and the Frères Jacques,

a quintessentially French singing quartet. In Saint-Germain today this tradition is carried on by the **café theatres**, whose tiny stages are usually surrounded by audiences jammed elbow to elbow. They offer a wide range of choice: singers and chansonniers, black humour, mime, strip-tease and plays by young authors. Most of these plays are soon forgotten, but there have been notable exceptions. Sixteen years ago two plays by a then unknown writer named Eugène Ionesco opened in a small theatre on the Left Bank. Today, more than 4,500 performances later, the two plays—*The Bald Prima Donna* and *The Lesson*—are still running; the scenery is now made of indestructible material, and the actors take each of the parts in turn.

Crossroads of Rue de Grenelle and Rue des Saints-Pères

In spite of the noise and the crowds in search of diversion, it should never be forgotten that people actually live in Saint-Germain-des-Prés, and to get to know the quarter properly the visitor must be ready to seek out and visit its **secret gardens** and quiet courtyards. Many of those who have spent a lifetime here no longer notice the noise, for although it is getting worse all the time, it is possible to ignore it with a little effort and practice. Whatever these old residents may secretly hope, it is unlikely that Saint-Germain will cease to be a fashionable quarter, for although the houses and apartments are inconvenient by modern standards, when one of them comes on the market there is always a queue of potential buyers. There are few modern buildings in the vicinity, and those which do exist, like the Faculty of Medicine in Rue des Saints-Pères, are becoming absorbed into the general scene. New and old residents alike turn out in force to shop at the Saint-Germain market, one of Paris's last covered markets, and jostle each other in true democratic fashion, as they make outspoken comments about the sweetness of a melon or the firmness of a Camembert. Like Rome as described by novelist Gore Vidal in Fellini's film *Roma*, Saint-Germain is a good place to wait for the end of the world. The motto under the cornice of an old **house in Rue des Saints-Pères** is still justified: Ici à jamais vive la joie de ta demeure—May the joy of thy dwelling live here forever.

Garden in courtyard, Rue Jacob

Donkeys on their way to the Luxembourg Gardens

The Luxembourg Gardens

The Luxembourg Gardens are Saint-Germain's oasis of open space. They belong to the Senate, which sits in the Luxembourg Palace, built for the Queen Mother, Marie de Médicis at the beginning of the 17th century by the architect Salomon de Brosse. The **Médicis fountain**, named after the Queen, was rebuilt in 1861 with stonework designed by the same architect. Carved in the niches of the fountain is the scene of the two mythical lovers Acis and Galatea surprised by Polyphemus—perhaps not an entirely suitable subject for a garden where children play.

A fine **formal flower garden** has been laid out under the windows of the Senate, and on the terraces of the gardens amusements have been provided for people of all ages.

For the children there is a roundabout with wooden horses, **donkeys** surrounded by children clamouring for a ride, and a puppet theatre. There are also bowling clubs, tennis courts, croquet lawns, and a bridge club to which—a revolutionary gesture—ladies were admitted for the first time in 1972, when a girl also won first place in the rigorous and highly competitive entrance examination to another traditional male preserve, the École Polytechnique. The orangery in the gardens housed Paris's museum of modern painting between 1886 and 1937, and there are plans for it to become the city's children's museum. No more appropriate place could be imagined.

Meanwhile, the gardens are themselves a museum of nineteenth-century French sculpture, including one of Carpeaux's major works, the *Fountain of the Four Quarters of the World*. Young contemporary sculptors also exhibit their works in the gardens, and the children play in and around the massive blocks of modern sculpture.

The Médicis fountain, Luxembourg Gardens

The square of Saint-Julien-le-Pauvre

Pillar of the ambulatory in the church of Saint-Séverin

The student quarter of Paris has been in the same place ever since the Middle Ages, although today there are only a few traces of the time when teaching was controlled and organized by the Church and was done in Latin. The narrow streets around the church of **Saint-Julien-le-Pauvre** do give some idea of what medieval Paris must have been like, but most of the memories of the period live on in street names. *Fouarre* is an old French word meaning straw, and Rue du Fouarre is a reminder of the time when students spread straw on the ground to sit on while their teacher lectured to them from a window. Rue de la Parcheminerie was the place where the students bought the books of rough parchment into which they copied out their textbooks, since the cost of a proper manuscript book was usually more than they could afford.

The church of Saint-Julien-le-Pauvre was built at the end of the 12th century, at the same time that Notre-Dame was being built on the other side of the river. This small rustic church was a resting place for pilgrims on their way from the North to St. James—"Saint-Jacques" to the French—of Compostella. The beginning of the route which they took as they set out for Spain from Saint-Julien-le-Pauvre is still called Rue Saint-Jacques. The university church of Saint-Séverin nearby is almost completely in flamboyant Gothic style. The plan of its double ambulatory is similar to that of Notre-Dame. The pointed arches branch out from a **pillar** which has the appearance of a fantastic palm tree.

Walking up Rue Saint-Séverin towards the top of the hill which the French, with some exaggeration, call a mountain—the Montagne Sainte-Geneviève—we pass the Hôtel de Cluny on our left, opposite the severe buildings of the Sorbonne. Built at the end of the 15th century as a residence for the abbots of the Benedictine abbey of Cluny in Burgundy, it is now a museum of life in medieval times. As well as interesting household utensils, it contains some wonderful late medieval tapestries, the finest of which is the set known as **The Lady with the Unicorn**.

According to legend, St. Genevieve became the patron saint of Paris by inspiring her fellow citizens with courage at the time of Attila's invasion in 451 A.D. The one remaining stone of her tomb can be seen in a reliquary in the church of Saint-Étienne-du-Mont, and

Detail from *The Lady and the Unicorn* tapestries, Cluny museum

church dates from the early 17th century and has a similar touch of fantasy, a mouthwatering hint of baroque bad taste.

The Panthéon was built in accordance with a vow made by Louis XV after recovering from a serious illness, and was designed by the architect Germain Soufflot in the neoclassical style which was then coming into fashion. The church was only dedicated to St. Genevieve for a short time, for in 1791 it was secularized, and as the Panthéon it became a burial ground for great men like Voltaire and Rousseau. It is still used for this purpose and the last big ceremony to be held there was in honour of the French Resistance hero Jean Moulin and other Resistance fighters. The interior is a mixture of different styles, reflecting the various uses to which the building has been put. The decoration is somewhat mediocre, apart from a series of paintings by Puvis de Chavannes depicting scenes from the life of St. Genevieve.

Two of France's most distinguished institutes of higher education, the École Normale Supérieure and the École Polytechnique, stand near to the top of the

Rue Soufflot on May Day, with the Panthéon beyond

was originally kept in a nearby sanctuary dedicated to her. The tower of this sanctuary forms part of the Henri IV lycée, once the home of the canons of Sainte-Geneviève, the protectors of the students who lived on the Montagne Sainte-Geneviève itself.

Saint-Étienne-du-Mont is a Renaissance church which has kept a fair amount of its original stained glass and some fine old paintings. Its most remarkable feature is its **rood screen**, which is the only one of its kind in Paris, where all the screens erected in medieval churches to separate the choir from the nave and prevent the congregation from seeing the Mass being performed have been destroyed. During the Counter Reformation, when the screen of Saint-Étienne-du-Mont was built, the idea was to incorporate a wide archway so that all of the choir could be seen. The carved figures which float at each side of the arch have the robust good health typical of French imitations of the Graces as rendered by Italian Renaissance sculptors. The **façade** of the

The church of Saint-Étienne-du-Mont

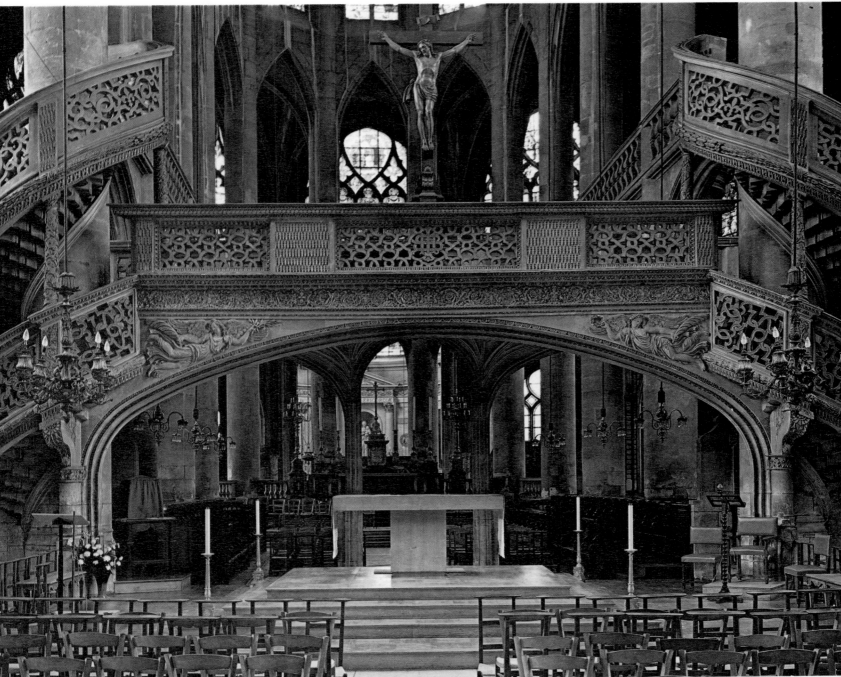

The rood screen of Saint-Étienne-du-Mont

Cages in the Jardin des Plantes

Montagne Sainte-Geneviève. The arts faculties are mostly on the hill itself, but as we walk down the eastern slope we enter the realm of the sciences. On the bank of the Seine is the Natural History Museum, where the various branches of the physical sciences are studied. The best-known part of the museum is the Jardin des Plantes, with its zoo where some of the original eighteenth-century **cages** and aviaries can still be seen. The appearance of the garden is an eloquent reflection of the age in which the Museum was created, an age in which scientists were burning with enthusiasm about the rapid growth of their knowledge of the universe. Two eighteenth-century buildings nearby—the house of Cuvier, one of the founding fathers of the science of paleontology, and an amphitheatre—are still in use. In the gardens there is a labyrinth above which rise the majestic branches of the first cedar of Lebanon to grow in Paris; it was brought to France by the great eighteenth-century botanist Bernard de Jussieu. In the 19th century, painters like Barye and Delacroix came to the Jardin des Plantes to draw the wild animals, and Henry Rousseau visited the tropical greenhouses to study the exotic plants which abound in his paintings, thus providing convincing evidence that he was the well-travelled man he claimed to be.

Since 1961 a new science faculty complex has been built on the riverside site where the old Wine Market used to be. The five-story rectangular blocks meeting at right-angles do not look particularly attractive from outside; they have been designed with functional requirements very much in mind. The various technical departments are on the two basement floors, and the staircases are in round towers at each corner. The whole complex is dominated by the **Zamanski tower** (named after the first dean of the new faculty), which contains the administrative offices. Twenty-seven stories and 300 feet high, its walls are decorated with mosaics by some of the contemporary artists who have worked on the decoration of the faculty buildings.

Right near to these modern buildings are the **Arenas of Lutetia** which, with the public baths near the Hôtel de Cluny, are the most important Gallo-Roman remains in Paris. Here, in what is with the Ile de la Cité the oldest part of Paris, we can grasp the extent of the city's importance in Roman times. The arena could hold 16,000 spectators—almost certainly more than the total population of Paris at that time. However, we know that the Gauls enthusiastically shared the Romans' enthusiasm for circus games, and the prospect of gladiatorial combat, exhibitions of wild animals, plays and other spectacles must have attracted many people from the surrounding countryside.

The Faculty of Sciences: the Zamanski tower

The arenas of Lutetia

3

SEVENTEENTH-CENTURY PARIS: THE MARAIS

Arcade in Place des Vosges

Le Marais—literally "the marsh"—is the oldest part of Paris to have kept its original appearance, for the good reason that it was divided up into building plots when durable construction materials were first starting to be widely used. The great age of the Marais was the 17th century, when the wealthiest section of French society owned magnificent "Hôtels"—town houses—there. Later the district's fortunes gradually declined, and it was abandoned to the poorer classes, the city's artisans and tradespeople, who left the warren of narrow streets and houses more or less as they found them. The new district began to be developed in the 14th and 15th centuries, when it lay behind the city ramparts built by King Charles V and also enjoyed the protection of the Bastille fortress. At this time, the French royal family was particularly fond of the Marais and owned property and houses there. The most sumptuous of these royal palaces, the fifteenth-century Hôtel des Tournelles, was abandoned by Catherine de Médicis in 1559 after the death of her husband, Henri II, from wounds received in a tournament held nearby.

At the beginning of the 17th century, Henri IV decided to promote the Marais as a residential district, and between 1604 and his death in 1610 he laid out a square lined with brick and stone houses of uniform design. Following a practice in his native province of the Béarn in southwest France he insisted that an arcade should run around the new square at street level to provide protection against the sun. Originally called Place Royale, the square was renamed **Place des Vosges** in 1799, in recognition of the promptness with which the Vosges administrative department had paid its taxes.

Aerial view of Place des Vosges

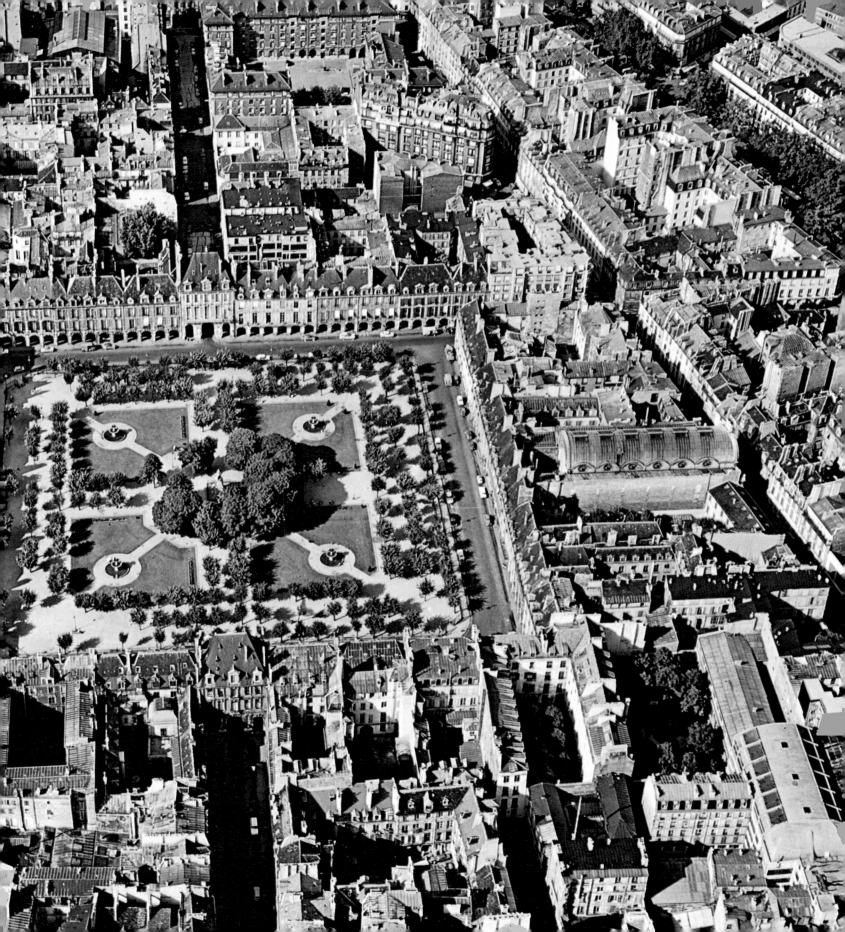

The Rue Saint-Antoine was the Marais's main thoroughfare. Today it is for the most part an undistinguished street, although a few traces of its former splendour have survived. These include: number 17, the seventeenth-century chapel of the Convent of the Visitation, built by the great architect François Mansart; the Hôtel de Mayenne at number 21; the Hôtel de Sully at number 62; and the church of St. Paul and St. Louis, where fashionable seventeenth-century ladies once flocked to hear the great preacher Louis Bourdaloue. French

Rue Saint-Antoine

Kings traditionally rode along Rue Saint-Antoine when they returned to Paris after being crowned at Rheims. The most splendid royal procession ever to pass through the Marais was Louis XIV's entry into Paris with his young bride Marie-Thérèse, after the Treaty of the

West front of the Hôtel de Sens

Courtyard of the Hôtel de Beauvais

Pyrenees in 1660. On that occasion, the Queen Mother and the states-man-prelate Cardinal Mazarin watched the procession go by from the balcony of the **Hôtel de Beauvais** in Rue François-Miron, whose oval courtyard is one of the best proportioned in Paris. The **Hôtel de Sens**, the oldest surviving town house in Paris, stands on the southern edge of the Marais, near to the Seine.

In 1634, Henri IV's great minister, the Duke of Sully, bought a magnificent house which had been built ten years earlier between Rue Saint-Antoine and Place Royale. Like most of the town houses in the Marais, the **Hôtel de Sully** does not look directly out onto the street, as was the practice in the Middle Ages. Instead, it has an entrance which is flanked by two slightly higher buildings and gives onto a courtyard. The main building stands at the end of this courtyard, while the wings on each side were originally the stables and kitchens. The architecture of the Hôtel de Sully is somewhat heavy, for Italian Renaissance ideas have been interpreted to suit French baroque taste: the windows are a little too close together; the allegorical figures representing the Elements and the Seasons are a little too squat; and although the exuberance of the decoration around the dormer windows is enjoyable, there is nevertheless something clumsy about it. The Hôtel has recently been restored by the French Historical Monuments Commission, which occupies it.

Experience has shown that the best way to preserve the old houses of the Marais is to find them some kind of cultural use. The beautiful seventeenth-century Hôtel Guénégaud, which is today occupied by a **Museum of Hunting and Nature**, is a good example of a building which has been restored and given a new lease of life in this way. Few of the original decorative fittings have survived in those buildings which are used as commercial

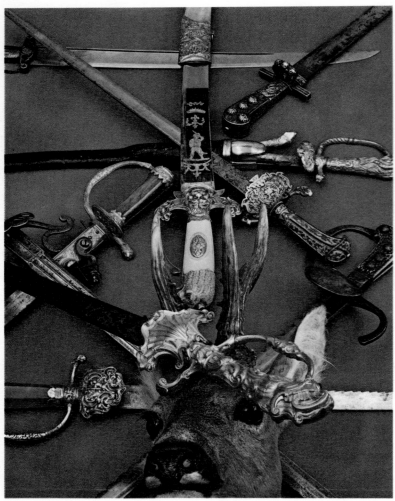

Seventeenth- and eighteenth-century weapons in the Hunting Museum.
Hôtel Guénégaud

The Hôtel de Sully

premises. Occasionally, during restoration work, a painted ceiling or a fine carved panel may be discovered beneath an undistinguished overlay, but this is a comparatively rare occurrence, and today many of the original decorative fittings of the Marais's Hôtels have either disappeared or have been transferred to museums. For this reason, houses like the Hôtel de Soubise and the Hôtel de Rohan, whose original decoration has survived, are particularly interesting.

The Hôtel de Soubise, often known as the Soubise Palace because of its palatial magnificence, was built by the architect Pierre-Alexis Delamair at the beginning of the 18th century, when French society was already beginning to desert the Marais for the broader streets of the Faubourg Saint-Germain district on the Left Bank of the Seine. Its façade illustrates how styles in urban architecture were changing at this time. Although its overall plan is similar to that of a seventeenth-century town house, the details and the proportions are quite different. The main buildings of the Hôtel de Soubise stand at the end of a vast oval courtyard framed by a portico which is a distant echo of Bernini's colonnade in St. Peter's Square in Rome. The volumes are elegantly emphasized by decorative carvings, and the slope of the roof, much less acute than in the previous century, is partly concealed behind a balustrade. The Museum of the History of France occupies the first floor, in rooms whose original wood panelling has been preserved, and the reading room of the French

The great courtyard of the Hôtel de Soubise

public record office, the Archives Nationales, is on the ground floor.

The Archives Nationales are also housed in the Hôtel de Rohan, which adjoins the Hôtel de Soubise. Also by Delamair, it was built for a cadet branch of the Rohan-Soubise family, which provided a line of Prince-Bishops of Strasbourg. Some of its fine rooms have survived, in particular the splendid **Cabinet des Singes**, whose panels are decorated with pastoral scenes framed by designs in which monkeys wearing clothes are shown in various lively and amusing postures. Behind a cupboard in the Cabinet des Singes, somewhat surprisingly in view of the decoration, is an oratory. Today the Hôtel de Rohan is often used for receptions and exhibitions.

The Cabinet des Singes in the Hôtel de Rohan

Ever since 1880, the Museum of the History of Paris has been housed in the Hôtel Carnavalet, which was built during the Renaissance and remodelled in the 17th century by François Mansart. Its most famous tenant was the Marquise de Sévigné, who lived there from 1677 until her death in 1696. The house still contains several portraits and objects belonging to her, although only one of the salons has survived from her time—a small room whose ceiling is decorated with painted beams. Other buildings have been added to the original nucleus of the museum, and various fragments of historic buildings and monuments have been reconstructed in the courtyards. Among them is the **Drapers' Pavilion,** which once stood in the Halles district not far away. Every aspect of life in old Paris is represented in the **Carnavalet Museum**. Particularly

Street signs in the Carnavalet Museum

remarkable is a collection of the street signs which, until about the time of the Revolution, when houses began to be numbered systematically, were used to indicate private dwellings as well as business premises. The museum also contains a number of exhibits from the Revolutionary period, including furniture used by members of the royal family in the Temple prison.

Opposite the Carnavalet Museum stands the Hôtel Lamoignon, which dates from the end of the 16th century and is one of the earliest examples in Paris architecture of the colossal order—whereby the ornamentation of a building is not compartmented story by story, but stretches as a unity through the whole height of the façade. It has been excellently restored, and is today occupied by the Historical Library of the City of Paris.

Nearer the Seine is another early seventeenth-century building, the **Arsenal**. Some of its old decoration has

The Drapers' Pavilion in the Hôtel Carnavalet

The Arsenal: Mme de la Meilleraye's Bedroom

survived: the bedroom and oratory of Mme de la Meilleraye, wife of a Marshal of France, date from the time
when the Arsenal was built, while the beautiful salons
go back to the time when the Duke of Maine,
Louis XIV's son by his mistress Mme de Montespan,
lived there as Grand Master of the Artillery. The
library was begun in the 18th century, and contains
some fine manuscripts. One of the most famous librar-
ians of the Arsenal was Charles Nodier, who held
a celebrated literary salon there in the early 19th century.
From 1824 on, he entertained at his home all the young
writers of the Romantic movement, and the staircase
once climbed by Alexandre Dumas, Victor Hugo,
Honoré de Balzac, Alfred de Musset, and many others
less well known, can still be seen today.

At a time when people generally felt much less senti-
mentally attached to the things of the past than they
do today, the original inhabitants of the Marais moved
without regrets to more modern houses elsewhere in
the city. The splendid but uncomfortable dwellings
they left behind them were adapted to the needs of new
and poorer tenants, most of whom were the **craftsmen**
of modest means who still form a sizeable proportion
of the quarter's population today.

Today the streets of the Marais are still as narrow
as they were then, and the houses are even further
removed from contemporary ideas of comfort. Nevertheless, many of them either have been or are currently
being restored at great expense. For the Marais has
come back into fashion with the very rich—or those
of the very rich who want a quiet and luxurious place
where they can get away from the modern world. At
the same time, the craftsmen and manual workers who
live in the quarter are finding it increasingly difficult to
make a living. They are being edged out of business
either because machines can do their work better or
else simply because there is less and less demand for
their kind of precision skills. Itinerant glaziers, carrying
sheets of glass, were once a familiar sight on the Paris
streets. Today their numbers are dwindling: glass is
tougher than it used to be, and it is anyway more
convenient to carry it in specially equipped vans or
trucks. The coal and wood merchants who traditionally
kept bars as part of their business are also disappearing,
victims of the growing popularity of oil-fired heating.

We can only hope against hope that new uses will be

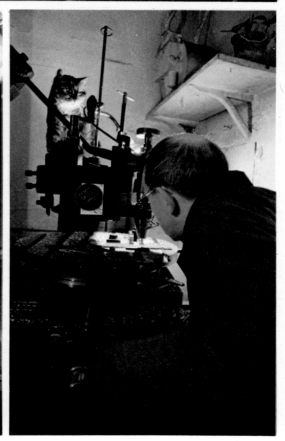

Tradesmen and craftsmen in the Marais

Hard at work beneath the July Column

dressed couples in search of something to warm them up and stave off the colds they had picked up at plays and concerts where the temperature had been lower than the courage of the performers—not to mention the audience. By now the tradespeople have got used to the festival, and many of them stay open late during June and July while it is on. Audience facilities have also improved: it is now possible to hire blankets to keep out the cold, and in wet weather shelter is provided. There is a wide range of entertainment—concerts, operas, classical and modern plays, and variety shows— and the overall standard is high. However, the Marais Festival has always been something of a gamble, if only because the Paris weather does not exactly encourage this kind of enterprise. Each year the Festival earns more bouquets than hard cash, and its future is constantly in jeopardy. It is to be hoped that it will

May Day parade, Place de la Bastille

found for craftsmen's skills in our rapidly changing world. The picture is not completely gloomy: for instance, there is still a need for fine needlework, and the watchmaker's skills are very much in demand. But for the string instrument repairers, the menders of porcelain and marquetry, and many of the other craftsmen who still live in the Marais, museums will soon be the only source of work.

Apart from restoration work, other attempts to bring new life to the Marais are being made. Since 1962, the organizers of the Marais Festival—many of whom give their services free—have been putting on outdoor shows in the courtyards of some of the quarter's fine houses. In the early years of the festival, bistro owners in the heart of the district were overwhelmed at festival time by a late-evening invasion of shivering, smartly continue to triumph over these financial difficulties.

President Pompidou gave his backing to another plan to bring life back to the Marais. This is the "Pompidou museum" of the twentieth-century arts which opened in Spring 1977 on the Plateau Beaubourg to the West of the Marais. The architects—English and Italian—were chosen after an international competition, and the plan was carried out in conjunction with the big redevelopment scheme for the Halles quarter, now that it is no longer the site of Paris's central food markets. Passionate debate is still going on about this development scheme, and for the time being all one can do is welcome an enterprise which may have its utopian aspects but is nevertheless a valid attempt to prevent the Marais from becoming a piously preserved historical monument, a beautiful necropolis insulated from the life of the modern world.

At the other end of the Marais from the Plateau Beaubourg is **Place de la Bastille**. The Bastille was a fortress built during the reign of Charles V in the 14th century to protect Paris against invasion from the East. It is usually thought of as a prison, but this is misleading because it was only a state prison for a relatively short time, during the 17th century, when Cardinal Richelieu was in power. Nevertheless, before the Revolution the Bastille became a symbol of the French King's arbitrary power—he had the right to imprison people by issuing "lettres de cachet," which exempted him from any need to justify himself before the courts. This explains why the capture of the Bastille by the people of Paris on July 14, 1789, was hailed as a great victory for the Revolution. The fact that there were only seven prisoners in the fortress at the time—four forgers, two madmen, and a rake who had been detained there at the request of his own family—did nothing to diminish the delight of the Paris mob. The Bastille was demolished, and its stones were used to build the Pont de la Concorde. Even today Place de la Bastille has an important place in revolutionary mythology and is an essential and symbolic port of call for most left-wing demonstrations and processions.

The fortress itself stood where the first houses of Rue Saint-Antoine stand today, and the outline of its towers can be seen marked out on the paving stones in the square. The Column in the centre of the square commemorates the Revolution of July 1830, when Louis-Philippe, the "Citizen King" of France, came to power. From the top of the 150-foot-high **July Column,** a bronze figure of the Spirit of Liberty surveys the square, a symbol of the passion for freedom which inspired the revolutionary tradition in France.

Scenes from the Marais Festival. Above: *I Turci Amanti* by Domenico Cimarosa at the Hôtel de Sully
Below: *Bacchianas* danced by New York's Harkness Ballet at the Hôtel de Rohan

4

THE PARIS OF THE KINGS: THE LOUVRE AND THE ROYAL SQUARES

Louvre Métro station

Originally a fortress which stood on the boundary of medieval Paris, the **Louvre** is today one of the world's greatest museums and art galleries. To put tourists into a receptive frame of mind and whet their aesthetic appetites, the Paris city transport authority has decorated the **Louvre Métro station** with casts of the works of art whose originals can be seen in the museum itself.

The Louvre did not become a museum until the Revolution. In the 16th and 17th centuries it was a royal palace, and later it housed academics and artists whose lodging was paid for by the King. The buildings which stretch to the Tuileries Gardens from the Louvre's inner courtyard, the Cour Carrée, were only completed during the reign of Napoleon III, the last French ruler to live in the Tuileries Palace, a country house built for Catherine de Médicis in the 16th century. The Palace ran at right angles to the Seine and stood between the Tuileries Gardens and the **Place du Carrousel**, the spacious courtyard which owes its name to celebrations held there in honour of the young King Louis XIV in 1662. It was burned down by the Commune in 1871. Had the Palace not been destroyed, today's magnificent view from the Place du Carrousel across the Tuileries to the Arc de Triomphe would not exist.

Time has bestowed a healing unity on the somewhat disparate buildings which line three sides of the Place du Carrousel. In 1964-65, France's then Minister of Culture, André Malraux, arranged for several bronze statues by the sculptor Aristide Maillol to be set out on the lawns of the square. Today their majestic forms fit admirably into this famous setting, while nearby, in the ground floor rooms of the Louvre gallery which overlooks the Seine, the visitor can see other, older statues—the flower of French sculpture from the Middle Ages to the 19th century.

Statue by Maillol in the gardens of Place du Carrousel

The Louvre is not one museum but several, each with its own needs in terms of space and organization. It is an unfortunate fact that these historic buildings are not ideally suited to their task, and the possibilities of adapting them to the varied requirements of specialized museum departments are limited.

The oldest part of the Louvre is the Cour Carrée, which stands on the site of the original fortifications. Its external appearance was changed in 1964, again on Malraux's instructions, when a deep trench was dug at the foot of the **Colonnade Façade** built by architect Claude Perrault between 1668 and 1678 to provide the Louvre Palace with an entrance on the city side. As a result of this the long classical portico has gained in lightness what it has lost in majesty. Balustrades and a bridge designed by French architect Jean Trouvelot from seventeenth-century drawings add to the effect and provide a noble approach to the courtyard. The Cour Carrée was built between the reigns of Henri II and Louis XIV, although each part of it fits into the grand design of the architect Pierre Lescot, who drew the plans in the Renaissance style inspired by the architecture of the Ancient World. Each building bears the monogram of the King in whose reign it was built. The **reliefs on the wall of the south side of the west façade** are the work of Jean Goujon, the greatest French sculptor of the 16th century, and in spite of restoration they have not lost the fluid grace typical of his work. Goujon also created the caryatids which support the musicians' gallery in the Salle des Caryatides, the fine room behind the west façade which today contains the Louvre's Greek sculpture collection.

Ever since the Louvre was first opened to the public as a museum on August 10, 1793, the arrangement of the collections has been to a large extent determined by the internal logic of the building. Sculpture is exhibited on the ground floor; paintings, objects and drawings on the floors above. Although the furniture of the period when the Louvre was a royal palace has disappeared, traces of the original ceilings have survived to influence the choice of certain rooms for certain collections. For example, the ancient statues of the Greek and Roman antiquities department go well with the classical style of the ceilings of Anne of Austria's summer apartment where they are housed, while the **Gallery of Apollo** provides an ideal setting for what is left of the French crown jewels.

The Louvre: Perrault's Colonnade Façade

The Louvre: reliefs on the west façade of the Cour Carrée

The Louvre: the Gallery of Apollo

Chance has played a considerable part in the assembling of the Louvre's collections of works of art. The royal collection seized by the state during the Revolution provided the nucleus; later came treasures confiscated from secularized monasteries, and the property of aristocrats who fled the country to escape the Revolution. Even at this early date the Louvre's most famous picture was Leonardo da Vinci's **Mona Lisa del Giocondo**, which everyone calls the "Mona Lisa," except the French, who call it "la Joconde." Not long ago an exhibition was held in Paris of photographs showing the reactions of people as they stood in front of it. The looks of surprise, if not of disappointment, to be seen on every face highlighted the irony of the Mona Lisa's great popular reputation; for it would be hard to imagine a work of art less capable of rewarding the first glance of the uninformed. Nevertheless, its popularity persists. During the hours when artists are allowed to copy paintings in the Louvre, there is always someone at work in front of the Mona Lisa—one of the many admirers of Leonardo's masterpiece who want to take away a less impersonal memento than a photograph.

The **Venus de Milo**, which stands on the ground floor in a room which was once Anne of Austria's bathroom, is another of the Louvre's star attractions. Some indication of the nature of its appeal can be gauged from the fact that it was once sent to Japan as a typical example of the art of Western civilization at one of its most glorious moments, when the Greeks saw in human beauty a reflection of the divine. Today we know that this statue of Aphrodite, discovered on the island of Melos in 1820 and bought by the French ambassador in Constantinople, is not a classical

The Louvre: the Mona Lisa

Greek work, as was once thought, but Hellenistic. But whatever the purists who dismiss Hellenistic art as decadent may think, the statue has the vigour of an original creation, and like the equally famous Winged

The Louvre: getting the right perspective

Victory of Samothrace, which was discovered over fifty years later and now stands on the landing of the great staircase leading to the upper stories of the Louvre, it gives visitors a powerful impression of idealized but still accessible beauty.

But there are other masterpieces in the Louvre, as well as these universally known works. Among them are Michelangelo's *Slaves*, Rubens's great series of paintings recording events in the life of Marie de Médicis, Van Eyck's *Madonna of Chancellor Rollin*, Vermeer's *Lacemaker*, and the *Hunts of Maximilian* series of tapestries. The Louvre collections provide a comprehensive record of the achievements of Western civilization and of the civilizations which have influenced its

The Louvre: The Venus de Milo

The Tuileries Gardens

Le Moulin de la Galette, by Auguste Renoir. Jeu de Paume Museum

The Concorde and the Arc de Triomphe from Arc de Triomphe du Carrousel

des Arts Décoratifs, which is in the wing of the building which runs along the Rue de Rivoli.

The **Tuileries Gardens** have been open to the public longer than any other gardens in Paris. By the early 17th century they were already a favourite meeting place for fashionable Parisians, although the gardens as we know them today were laid out by the great landscape gardener Le Nôtre in 1664. In the 19th century, when

development; the art of ancient Mesopotamia and Egypt, for example, is generously represented. Finally, the museum contains the finest collection of postmedieval French painting in the world.

Owing to the requirements of modern methods of presentation, today there is not enough space in the Louvre for all the collections to be displayed in their entirety. Since 1947, for example, the French national collection of Impressionist paintings has been housed in the Jeu de Paume museum at the opposite end of the Tuileries Gardens to the Louvre. Working in the face of bitter adverse criticism from the public, the Impressionists helped to lay the foundations of modern art. They liberated nineteenth-century painting from the stultifying influence of academic teaching and found inspiration in the observation of everyday life. Through the generosity of discriminating collectors, the Jeu de Paume contains many of their finest paintings. In this light and airy museum, the eye moves easily to the trees outside and then back again to the Impressionists' vision of nature. **Le Moulin de la Galette** was painted by Renoir in 1876, and sums up many of the things the Impressionists were trying to do. It was, for instance, painted out of doors—in the garden of a popular dance hall in Montmartre, where the artist recruited his models by giving them hats decorated with red ribbon according to the latest fashion. The radiance and optimism which are the hallmark of Renoir's vision fill the room where his pictures are hung in the Jeu de Paume.

The Jeu de Paume contains the work of painters like Cézanne, Van Gogh and Gauguin who have had a profound influence on twentieth-century art and whose great creative period was before 1900. Contemporary art and the latest work in design are to be found in another museum in the Louvre complex—the Musée

The Arc de Triomphe du Carrousel and the Tuileries Gardens

the rulers of France lived in the Tuileries Palace, only one part of the gardens was set apart for them. The entrance to this was near the small **Arc de Triomphe du Carrousel**, which was built for Napoleon I by the architects Percier and Fontaine in 1808. The horses which pull the triumphal car on top of the arch, which is an imitation of the arch of Septimius Severus in Rome, were originally those taken from St. Mark's, Venice, as part of the plunder of the Italian campaigns. These

The Orangerie Museum: one of the rooms containing the *Nymphéas* by Claude Monet

were reclaimed by the Austrians in 1815 and replaced by copies. The disappearance of the Tuileries Palace has created an odd resonance between the Arc de Triomphe du Carrousel and its bigger counterpart at the top of the Champs-Élysées, which was built later.

Opposite the Jeu de Paume, on the terrace beside the Seine, stands the Orangerie museum, which has recently been equipped to house temporary exhibitions. At the far end of the Orangerie, a group of rooms has been set aside for a permanent exhibition of Monet's **Nymphéas**, the studies of waterlilies on the pond of his country home at Giverny which the painter executed towards the end of his life. In 1923 he presented some of them to the French nation, and today the circular rooms of the Orangerie in which they hang are to Monet's art what the Sistine chapel is to Michelangelo's. In these great paintings Monet had moved on from his early attempts to capture the impression of a moment. Like his contemporary, Cézanne, whose artistic development was otherwise quite different, he had achieved a form of expression bordering on abstraction.

The **terrace of the Tuileries Gardens** provides an ideal vantage point over the Place de la Concorde, which the French poet Louis Aragon has somewhat optimistically called the cleanest place in the world. Whatever the truth of Aragon's claim, the square certainly does seem to have been thought out by a tidy mind. In 1748, when the architect Jacques-Ange Gabriel drew the plans for Louis XV, after whom the square was named, the site lay between the Tuileries Gardens and open country.

Place de la Concorde seen from the terrace of the Tuileries Gardens

One of the fountains on Place de la Concorde

A contemporary wrote that the Place Louis XV was "the way into the city for travellers who come from the province of Normandy," and then went on to hazard the opinion that "it will be much used." He could hardly have imagined just how far his prediction would come true. The square only assumed its final form in the 19th century, when the ditches around it were filled in and the Obelisk of Luxor was erected in the centre, replacing the original monument to Louis XV, which had been melted down during the Revolution. On January 16, 1793, the guillotine was set up on the square for the execution of Louis XVI, and it remained there throughout the Reign of Terror. In an attempt to obliterate these gruesome memories, the square was renamed **Place de la Concorde** by the Convention, the revolutionary assembly which ruled France between September 1792 and October 1795.

The two colonnaded buildings which give onto the square were also built by Gabriel. The one on the left is simply a façade added to the buildings behind, and the other, which is now France's Ministry of the Navy, was originally the royal furniture store. The obelisk stands at the centre of a north-south axis formed by the church of the Madeleine and the National Assembly on the other side of the river. The **fountains** on Place de la Concorde were designed by the nineteenth-century French architect Hittorf. On the eastern and western sides of the square rise the leafy trees of the Tuileries Gardens and the Champs-Élysées, counterbalancing the undulations of the Paris skyline to the North, which is dominated by the white cupolas of the Sacré-Cœur from their perch on the crest of the hill of Montmartre. The centuries have combined to create a sense of order on Place de la Concorde. With the passing of time, the various elements—the most unusual of which is certainly the obelisk dedicated to Ramses II around 1250 B.C.— have formed a unity, so that today it is hard to isolate its constituent parts.

Place de la Concorde, with the church of the Madeleine beyond

Place Vendôme
and the Vendôme column

The Place de la Concorde is connected to the Louvre on its south side by the quays, on the north by the **Rue de Rivoli**, which was built on the orders of Napoleon when he was First Consul. To clear the approaches to the Tuileries Palace, where he was then living, Napoleon decided that the new street should be twenty yards wide. Work began in 1803, and two years later the Rue de Rivoli was paved and lit. The houses which line the street took longer to build, because they had to conform to specifications for the beautification of the city drawn up by Percier and Fontaine. These specifications were for three-storied houses with sloping roofs, and an Italian-style arcade at street level. Only the Hôtel de Talleyrand, on the corner of Rue Saint-Florentin, was exempted from this rule. From the very beginning the street was conceived of as a prestige shopping area. Trades involving the use of an oven were banned; there were no bakers' shops on the Rue de Rivoli. The prestige shops are still there. Today, the Rue de Rivoli and its neighbouring streets still attract visitors to Paris in search of souvenirs of their visit—picture postcards, guidebooks, ties, jewellery and so on.

The Rue de Castiglione leads off from the Rue de Rivoli to another of Paris's royal squares. Originally known as the Place des Conquêtes, this square was planned in 1687 and built on land belonging to the Hôtel de Vendôme, whose name it has since taken. The appearance of the **Place Vendôme** was changed when a column covered with bronze from the 1,200 cannon captured from the Russians and Austrians at the Battle of Austerlitz was erected there in honour of Napoleon's armies. Built on the same lines and with the same purpose as Trajan's column in Rome, the Vendôme column is crowned by a statue of Napoleon, suitably dressed in Roman costume. The 143-foot-high column dominates the square's fine classical buildings designed by Jules Hardouin-Mansart. The Ministry of Justice occupies the central building on the western side, and the air of gravity and dignity which it brings to the square is maintained by its next-door neighbour, the Ritz Hotel. The Place Vendôme was once a meeting place for the veterans of Napoleon's armies, who came to exchange reminiscences at the foot of the massive bronze column carved with the record of victories over which, Balzac said, Napoleon is keeping watch.

Royal squares are usually among

Rue de Rivoli and its arcades

the earliest victims of revolutions: Louis XIV's Place des Conquêtes became a monument to the glory of Napoleon, and the guillotine claimed its victims on Place Louis XV. The Place des Victoires had a somewhat happier fate. It has retained its original name, and the statue of Louis XIV which stands in the middle of the square today is no less regal and majestic than the one

Stone mask in Place des Victoires

around which it was built. The original statue of
Louis XIV was commissioned by an ardent courtier,
the Duc de la Feuillade, as the centrepiece of the square,
which in the late 17th century contained bas-reliefs
depicting great events in the King's life. Dispersed during the Revolution, some of these reliefs eventually
found their way into the English royal collection, whence
they were returned to France by King George V in 1914.
Today they are in the Louvre, and the only reminders
of the age of Louis XIV in **Place des Victoires** are the
equestrian statue of the Sun King which dates from
shortly after the restoration of the French monarchy
in 1815, and the **masks** which smile down from above
the arches of houses built by Jules Hardouin-Mansart.

Place des Victoires stands almost on the edge of the
district which contains great institutions such as the
Bank of France, the stock exchange, and France's equiv-
alent of the British Museum or the Library of Congress,
the Bibliothèque Nationale. The library occupies the
building which was once the residence of Cardinal
Mazarin. Some of the original decoration has survived,
and it is often used to create settings for exhibitions of
the work of writers and artists whose work is kept in
the library's various departments. Just outside this district, a stone's throw from Place des Victoires, is Les
Halles, the commercial quarter which until a few years
ago was the site of the city's central food markets.

Walking back towards the Seine, we cross the gardens
of the Palais-Royal, which is lined with houses built
in 1781 as a speculative operation by the Duke of
Orleans, who was later to earn the nickname "Égalité"
for his egalitarian ideas during the Revolution—at
that time it was considered scandalous for a Prince of
the blood to get involved in the construction business.
The Palais-Royal was originally the palace of Cardinal
Richelieu, who bequeathed it to the royal family.

THE LOUVRE AND THE ROYAL SQUARES

Place des Victoires

Fountain in Place du Théâtre-Français,
with the theatre building in the background

Louis XIV spent his childhood there, and then gave it to his brother, the Duke of Orleans, whose descendant transformed it a century later. Looking at this quiet square today, it is hard to imagine that it had a dubious reputation in the late 18th century and the early 19th, when the cafés beneath the arcades provided a favourable atmosphere for assignations, and the gaming houses attracted a shady clientele. Today the square's main attraction is its peaceful atmosphere, broken only by the shouts of children at play. The writers Colette and Jean Cocteau spent the closing years of their lives here.

On the corner of Rue de Valois, which forms one side of the Palais-Royal, stood a theatre whose first tenant was Molière, who died at his home in the nearby Rue de Richelieu on February 17, 1673, after the fourth performance of the *Malade Imaginaire*. The chair in which he acted that night was kept by the troupe, and eventually found its way to the theatre on the other side of the Palais-Royal gardens which has been the headquarters of the actors of **the Comédie-Française** since 1799. The new building had been designed by the architect Victor Louis, who also built the theatre of Bordeaux, to replace Molière's original theatre, which had been burned down some years before.

The actors are still there today, although the company is bigger than it was in Molière's time, and the **Théâtre Français building** is now too small to contain the complex organization which the troupe requires. Nevertheless they are attached to the building in which many of them spend most of their professional lives, surrounded by mementoes of their illustrious predecessors. In the foyer Jean-Antoine Houdon's bust of **Voltaire**, presented to the Comédie-Française by his niece in memory of the triumphal evening which the company staged in her uncle's honour, smiles down on the theatre-goers. It was once suggested that he is smiling at the nonsense he hears people talking.

The Comédie-Française has a faithful public willing to stand and queue in all weathers for half an hour before every performance in order to buy the seats in the pit near to the stage, which are still cheap as a reminder of the time when the audience stood in that part of the theatre. However, the company has recently been trying hard to attract a wider range of people than their traditional audience by staging modern plays. But one thing has not changed: the standard of acting is as high as ever it was, for even the smallest parts are always given to experienced actors.

The theatre of the Comédie-Française: Houdon's Voltaire in the gallery of busts

A performance at the Comédie-Française

5

EIGHTEENTH-CENTURY PARIS: THE FAUBOURG SAINT-GERMAIN

The Champ-de-Mars seen from the Eiffel Tower, with the École Militaire beyond

In 1670, when Louis XIV decided to build the Hôtel des Invalides, as a place where the veterans of his army could enjoy a well-earned retirement, he chose a site west of the abbey of Saint-Germain-des-Prés and the area outside the medieval city walls which was known as the Faubourg Saint-Germain. During the 18th century, the population of the Faubourg gradually increased, and when Louis XV came to found the **École Militaire** in 1751, to train officers for the royal army, he built it even further to the West. Today these two fine classical buildings give their neighbourhood in the 7th Arrondissement its keynote of dignity and austerity; there are few elegant shops and casual strollers in the broad avenues of this part of Paris, for the main business of the district is official, not commercial, and its most striking modern landmark is the headquarters of UNESCO. Indeed, when it was completed in 1958, the UNESCO building was considered by many to be scandalously modernistic and out of keeping with its immediate surroundings. Today, however, it is well on the way to being absorbed into the prevailing atmosphere, the special flavour, of this part of the 7th Arrondissement, a powerful mixture of nobility and a certain gloom which is after all not inappropriate to a district where the historic exploits of the French army are commemorated and its future leaders trained.

Built between 1679 and 1706, the church of **Saint-Louis-des-Invalides** is a magnificent example of the noble and majestic style characteristic of

The dome of the Invalides

Louis XIV's architect Jules Hardouin-Mansart. All the artists who were working on the royal palace then being built at Versailles were mobilized to decorate the interior of what is today the most beautiful baroque church in Paris. Saint-Louis-des-Invalides stands comparison with St. Paul's cathedral in London; for the plans for the two churches have several points in common, perhaps because they were both influenced by the same model, St. Peter's in Rome. The dome of the Invalides curves the most steeply of the three, as it rises lightly above

Napoleon's tomb

was used throughout, and the only touch of colour is provided by the marble marquetry floor, the work of French craftsmen who used an Italian technique brought to France by Louis XIV's great trade minister, Colbert. In the 19th century part of this magnificent floor was removed to make room for **Napoleon's tomb**.

In his will, Napoleon expressed a wish to be buried on the banks of the Seine. However, he died in exile on the Atlantic island of St. Helena, on May 5, 1821, and was buried there. In 1840, King Louis-Philippe carried out Napoleon's request; the Emperor's remains were solemnly brought back to France, where they were laid in a monumental sarcophagus of red porphyry and set in an open crypt which had been dug beneath the dome of the Invalides. Twelve statues of Victory by the nineteenth-century sculptor James Pradier line the walls around the crypt and keep watch over the tomb. The overall effect is cold, but this does not discourage the many thousands of tourists from all over the world who flock to the Invalides each year in order to pay their respects to France's most famous ruler.

Along the right-hand side of the church of the Invalides, looking towards the Seine, a passage leads

Flags in the Musée de l'Armée

the solid, two-story portico of the façade. Inside the church the decoration is a remarkable and totally successful attempt to glorify the French monarchy; it also brings out the perfect proportions of the building, which was conceived around the central dome, with a rotunda at each of the corners. White stone with a texture as smooth as marble to the Hôtel des Invalides, where invalid soldiers still live today, as they did in the 17th century. The Hôtel was built around a series of quadrangles by the architect Libéral Bruant. The severity of the buildings brings to mind simultaneously the monastery and the barracks. The **rectangular central courtyard** of the Hôtel des Invalides is surrounded by a two-story, cloisterlike gallery, and the staircase steps are shallow so that the wounded soldiers who lived in the building could climb them more easily. The gallery walls are hung with plaques commemorating heroic actions by French troops. On the left-hand side of the main courtyard are the buildings of the Musée de l'Armée, whose exhibits illustrate the history of weapons and military equipment from the Middle Ages to our own times. The layout of the museum has recently been reorganized, and each day visitors file through the new rooms, admiring the armour of François I, or pausing for thought before the **tattered flags** which are the trophies of victorious campaigns.

The Hôtel des Invalides: the central courtyard

"The Kiss" by Auguste Rodin, in the garden of the Rodin Museum

"The Gate of Hell" by Rodin

If we leave the Invalides by the side which looks out towards the Seine, we have a fine, uncluttered view of the long rectangular façade, with the dome of the royal chapel rising above it. The approach to this façade is flanked by ditches, beside which stand eighteenth-century cannon brought back from Vienna by Napoleon, and two tanks captured by French troops in World War II.

Turning east from the Invalides we enter the Faubourg Saint-Germain proper, where the French aristocracy built their town houses during the 18th century. Of the hundred or so houses built in the quarter between 1700 and 1790, many are now embassies or government offices, and consequently difficult to visit. However the Hôtel Peyrenc de Moras, *is* open to the public because it houses the **Rodin Museum**. The house is rectangular in shape, like a typical eighteenth-century French château, with projecting parts which subtly enliven the bareness of the façades. It was gradually stripped of its interior fittings by successive owners and was more or less a shell by 1917, when it became a museum of the work of the great sculptor Auguste Rodin, who once had a studio in it.

"Attila reducing Italy and her arts to barbarism" by Eugène Delacroix
the library ceiling of the Palais-Bourbon

At the time when Rodin lived in the Hôtel, its other tenants included the dancer Isadora Duncan, Henri Matisse, Jean Cocteau, and the Austrian poet Rainer Maria Rilke, who became a great admirer of the sculptor's work. Today this is displayed inside the Hôtel and, in the case of monumental sculptures too big to fit in the rooms, outside in the garden. Among the outstanding exhibits which can be seen at the museum is the model for *The Gate of Hell*, commissioned for the Musée des Arts Décoratifs and never finished, although Rodin worked on it for thirty years. It provides a glimpse of a tortured, tormented world peopled by writhing forms representing the sufferings and aspirations of the human condition. In the centre, dominating the whole scene, is Rodin's famous statue, *The Thinker*. Other aspects of Rodin's wonderfully vigorous talent are illustrated by such fine works as *The Kiss* and *The Burghers of Calais*.

Rue de Bourgogne leads from the Rodin Museum to the **Palais-Bourbon,** known today as the Assemblée Nationale, the seat of the Deputies who constitute the lower house of the French legislature. Only the façade of the south courtyard has survived of the original Palais-Bourbon, which was a town house built for the Duchesse de Bourbon between 1722 and 1728. On the eve of the Revolution, her grandson, the Prince de Condé, carried out extensive alterations to the building, and added to it the Hôtel de Lassay, which stands on the quay of the Seine and is today the official residence of the President of the Assemblée Nationale. The neoclassical houses on Place du Palais-Bourbon date from the same period. A statue representing *The Law* was put up in the centre of the square in 1855, to symbolize the fact that the Palais-Bourbon had become the seat of the

THE FAUBOURG SAINT-GERMAIN

French legislature. The building had been seized by the nation during the Revolution, and in 1795 it became the meeting place of the Council of 500, which formed part of the legislature at that time. A debating room looking out onto the river was built, and in 1807 the purely decorative classical façade was added to harmonize with that of the Madeleine, the Temple of Glory which Napoleon was then building on the opposite side of the river in honour of his army. The architecture of the Deputies' debating hall and the rooms around it, which were built by the architect Jules de Joly between 1828 and 1832, is somewhat solemn and ponderous. However, some of the finest nineteenth-century painting in Paris is to be seen on the **library ceiling** of the Assemblée Nationale, where Delacroix executed a series of pictures between 1838 and 1847. In the pendentives around each of the five small domes which form the library ceiling, Delacroix's paintings depict the history of the civilization of the ancient world from its origins, seen through the benefits conferred on society by art, to its end through the

The façade of the Palais-Bourbon looking out over the Pont de la Concorde

The Hôtel Matignon

evils of war. Thus one of the paintings shows *Orpheus bringing civilization to the Greeks*, while the subject of the final picture in the series is *Attila reducing Italy and her arts to barbarism*. As a rule only members of the legislature are allowed to visit the library, but it is possible to get special permission. The public can also attend sessions of the Chamber of Deputies, although it is as well to remember that the visitors' galleries are usually packed during important debates.

The Faubourg Saint-Germain is still a quiet residential district, just as it was when the French aristocracy moved there in the 18th century, after abandoning their cramped houses in the Marais across the river. In 1704 the city authorities drew up plans for avenues to be built across the Faubourg, in order to join it to the city proper. When trying to imagine what the district looked like at that time we should think in terms of a loose mosaic of fine houses like the **Hôtel de Chanaleilles**, with gaps between them which were later filled with apartment buildings. A large number of the older

houses have survived. They were built as pavilions standing between an outer courtyard and a garden, the courtyard being lined with outbuildings and dependencies such as stables, kitchens, and a porter's lodge. Thus the visitor who wants to see the elegant façades of the town houses of the Faubourg Saint-Germain must be ready to penetrate beyond the often-forbidding walls of these former dependencies which give directly on to the street. Many of the houses still have their own fine parks, and that belonging to the **Hôtel Matignon**, the French Prime Minister's official residence, is the biggest private garden in Paris.

In 1760, the French architect and engraver Pierre Patte wrote as follows: "In the past, people chose their accommodation simply for effect; they knew nothing about the art of making a comfortable home for its own sake. All the pleasant arrangements which people admire in modern houses and which make modern houses so delightful to live in have only been invented in our time." There is a lot of truth in this. As far as the art of living

Garden in a courtyard, Rue de Sèvres

The Hôtel de Chanaleilles

is concerned, the Middle Ages seem to have lingered on until the 18th century. Only then did the various rooms of a house begin to be used for different purposes; hitherto a house had been simply a group of rooms whose functions were interchangeable. In the 18th century, too, furniture designers began to produce work which was something more than a variation on the theme of the all-purpose medieval coffer, which had held sway for so long. Even Versailles, it should be remembered, had been built to all intents and purposes as a medieval palace; no concessions had been made to the idea of comfort. And so when the aristocracy moved into the Faubourg Saint-Germain, they wanted to bring to their new homes that refinement in the art of living which was missing at court. Thus began the tradition of gracious living which we still think of as typical of eighteenth-century life, for the rich at any rate.

A great deal of building went on in the **Faubourg Saint-Germain** during the first quarter of the 18th century, when rococo was at the height of fashion. Although architectural structure continued to be restrained, ornamental details blossomed, as we can see in the mannered decorative features of the earliest houses in the Faubourg. Masks smile on window fasteners; naked figures curve and entwine around doorknockers; carved foliage and shells fit into cornices and soften the bareness of the stone. The later houses—those built between about 1750 and the Revolution—are characteristic of the early neoclassical style: the lines are still severe, and the effect is nobler, though less agreeable, than in those built earlier. During this period, most of the French ruling class lived in the Faubourg Saint-Germain. They were art-lovers, and they filled their houses with furniture, objets d'art, paintings, and curios, many of which were seized and sold when their owners fled to escape the Revolution. Later occupants of the Faubourg were left with only the bare architectural bones of the houses to remind them of the life-style of the eighteenth-century aristocracy. Some members of the French nobility did actually return to the Faubourg in the 19th century, but in many cases they moved into new houses: the most palatial of the existing ones had been taken over by the state. Some members of the new Imperial aristocracy also came to live in these peaceful streets where there were—and still are—fewer shops than anywhere else in Paris. The houses of the Faubourg Saint-Germain have had a happier fate than those of the Marais: they have never really gone down in the world. In the 19th century, for example, the Faubourg was still highly fashionable, as the novels of Balzac and Proust reveal. Its image of conservative refinement enabled it to hold its own successfully against the new residential districts

Ornamental details in the Faubourg Saint-Germain: Above left: The Hôtel d'Aligre, 15, Rue de l'Université; centre: the Hôtel du Président Duret, 67, Rue de Lille; right: the Hôtel de Gouffier de Thoix, 56 Rue de Varenne. Below left: 19 Rue de Lille; centre: the Hôtel Matignon; right: 13 Rue de Lille

which were being developed on the Right Bank of the Seine around Place Vendôme, the Chaussée d'Antin and the Faubourg Saint-Honoré.

The 7th Arrondissement has kept something of its traditional character. There are still many private houses in it with gardens flourishing behind unfriendly walls; a few fronds of greenery can sometimes be seen from the street, the only sign of their existence to the outside world. The Marais is coming back into fashion in a big way, it is true. Nevertheless, the Faubourg Saint-Germain still has its devotees among those who prize peace and quiet above all else, and those who either want to get away from the noise and bustle of Saint-Germain-des-Prés or else cannot find anywhere to live there. This is why people like the novelist Julien Green have chosen to live in a district which admittedly lacks the surface attraction of nearby Saint-Germain-des-Prés, yet does have a special charm of its own, that of a large but somewhat provincial city.

The present occupants of the great eighteenth-century houses usually try to preserve the original interior decoration as far as they can. The **Hôtel de Beauharnais,** one of the finest buildings in the Faubourg, is a good example of this zeal for preservation. Built in 1713 by the architect Germain Boffrand for his own use, it was bought in 1803 by Napoleon's stepson, Prince Eugène de Beauharnais, who built an Egyptian-style portico in the courtyard, in accordance with the avant-garde taste of the day. The rooms of the Hôtel de Beauharnais are also an example (and a rare one, since most of the houses lived in by members of Napoleon's family have not survived) of the mania for the Ancient World which swept France during the First Empire. As for the **Turkish bedroom**, it illustrates in a particularly striking way the eclecticism which resulted from the impact of early Romanticism on traditional French taste. However, the way in which the decor is organized shows the influence of the still dominant neoclassical style.

Built in 1770, the **Hôtel du Châtelet** is a fine example of early neoclassicism. The beautiful **grand staircase**, unlike those found in later buildings, does not give

The Turkish bedroom in the Hôtel de Beauharnais

an impression of glacial bareness. The banister may lack the soft outline and various other marks of rococo decoration characteristic of early eighteenth-century staircases, but even so its pure lines form a perfect harmony with the fluted pilasters and replicas of classical statues which stand in the niches.

It is usually impossible to get permission to look around the great mansions of the Faubourg which have been taken over by French government departments. However, those who want to visit a late eighteenth-century town house should go to the Hôtel de Salm on Quai Anatole-France. Built in 1782, it houses the Grand Chancellery of the Legion of Honour, and in a modern wing of the building is a museum devoted to the history of French orders of chivalry. The Hôtel de Salm has a courtyard with a monumental portico giving onto Rue de Lille, while its terrace overlooking the Seine is dominated by a circular pavilion with a flattened dome unexpectedly surrounded by a group of statues.

As we walk along the Seine from the Hôtel de Salm towards Notre-Dame, the Louvre comes into view on

Staircase of the Hôtel du Châtelet, today occupied by France's Ministry of Labour

Booksellers on the quays of the Seine

Bookseller at work

the opposite side of the river. We pass the Pont-Royal, built in 1685 to provide a crossing opposite the Tuileries Palace and to replace the ferry which had crossed the river at that point and is still remembered in the name of a nearby street: Rue du Bac—"Ferry Street." Quai Voltaire provides a reminder that the great philosopher died here on the corner of Rue de Beaune, in a house belonging to his disciple, the Marquis de Villette. A statue of Voltaire was recently erected in the square on Rue de Seine immediately behind the **palace of the Institut de France**, the most outstanding building on the banks of the Seine opposite the Louvre.

The history of the building is as follows. The seventeenth-century statesman Cardinal Mazarin left provision in his will for the foundation of a college to educate sixty students from Artois, Alsace, Roussillon and Pignerol, the four provinces which became part of France by the terms of the Treaty of the Pyrenees in 1660. The so-called College of the Four Nations was built between 1665 and 1687 from plans by the architect Louis Le Vau. The aerial photograph shows the magnificent semicircular façade and the austere buildings in the courtyards behind, where the students lived. The focal point of the buildings is the oval dome of the chapel, which for many years contained its founder's tomb. The tomb finally ended up in the Louvre, where it stayed until recently, when an agreement was made between the Louvre and the Institut de France, which today occupies Mazarin's college, to return it to its former resting place in the chapel. Today the chapel is used for the formal

meetings of the five academies—the most famous of which is the Académie Française—which make up the Institut de France. New members of the Académie Française are received beneath the dome. These reception ceremonies attract large numbers of people eager to hear the new Academician, wearing the green-embroidered uniform designed when the Institut was reorganized in 1795, make the traditional speech in praise of his predecessor, while his own career is described by another member of the Académie. The demand for invitations to these ceremonies always exceeds supply, but people who apply to the Institut for tickets for the opening session of the year, when the ceremonial is similar, are less likely to be disappointed. The members of the five academies are co-opted, and their choice does not fully reflect progressive movements in the arts, if only because the mavericks of the literary and artistic worlds often find Academic (in both senses of the word) discipline repugnant. Meanwhile, although there are no longer any residential students in Mazarin's college, its magnificent library in the eastern wing of the pavilion continues to attract large numbers of scholars.

The **booksellers** ply their traditional trade on the quays near the Institut. Their boxes of secondhand books and engravings contain plenty of oddities, but nowadays exceptional finds are rare. Anatole France, who lived on the quay, was once given the artist David's sketchbook of Napoleon's coronation by his publisher, Sergent, who had found it in a bookseller's twopenny box. Today the booksellers do not make such mistakes. Although the experts may have deserted them, they still have a faithful following of customers who would rather rummage through their boxes than visit a bookshop and are happy to rescue the attic castaways which find their way to the quays.

Aerial view of the Institut de France

6

NINETEENTH-CENTURY PARIS: THE RIGHT BANK

Detail of the Pont Alexandre III

The visitor to Paris who steps out of the Invalides air terminal, a building which might well be the orangery of a French château, and looks up and down the broad esplanade which stretches from the Hôtel des Invalides to the Seine cannot fail to be struck by the curious way in which the grey light of Paris somehow imposes a kind of unity on the most disparate pieces of architecture. At one end of the esplanade stands the Hôtel des Invalides itself, which dates from the late 17th century; at the other is the ornamental ironwork of the **Pont Alexandre III**, a bridge which was built in the closing years of the 19th century. The group formed by the bridge and the Grand Palais and the Petit Palais on the other side of the river is highly typical of what the French call "1900 style." The richness and exuberance of the decoration fail to conceal its lack of any real inspiration, and the style itself diverts attention from the real innovation of the period, which was in structural techniques. The foundation stone of the bridge, which crosses the Seine with a single 350-foot-long span, was laid by Tsar Nicholas II in 1896, although it was named after his father, Alexander III. The functional purpose of the metal girders is effectively concealed beneath the lavish ornamentation, whose splendour rings a little hollow. On top of the pylons at each corner of the bridge is a gilded statue of an allegorical figure, and at the bottom there are groups of Cupids and lions which are as gratuitous as the decoration of a Bavarian rococo church.

The Pont Alexandre III and the Invalides

Between the Pont Alexandre III and the Grand and the Petit Palais, which face one another across Avenue Churchill, is the Cours-La-Reine, a chestnut-covered walk which was laid out by Queen Marie de Médicis in 1616. The Petit Palais, on the right, was built as a museum in 1900. This extremely adaptable building is the permanent home of the city of Paris's collection of ancient art and from time to time houses big temporary exhibitions. The **Grand Palais**, opposite, was built with less definite aims in view. It is a mélange of architectural styles: there is a monumental loggia in the Ionic order, its inside wall covered with a glass mosaic depicting the great ages of art; the **porch,** which belongs to no particular school; and sculptures on the façade which reflect Art Nouveau at its most convoluted. However, even the most biased judge has to admit that the triumphal chariots at each corner of the building are a tour de force of technical skill. No two façades of the Grand Palais are exactly alike, though each has its share of wildly gesticulating carved figures. Inside, however, it is a different story. Many exhibitions had been held beneath the 140-foot-high glass **dome** of the Grand Palais by 1959, the year when French Minister of Culture André Malraux decided to justify the inscription carved on the façade—"Building dedicated by the Republic to the glory of French art"—by transforming it into a kind of multipurpose cultural centre. The work was entrusted to Reynold Arnould, who built France's first Maison de la Culture in 1961 and was already well known as a museum designer.

Since 1937, the west wing of the Grand Palais has been occupied by Paris's science museum, the Palace of Discovery, where visitors can keep up with the latest scientific developments and see demonstrations of the great scientific discoveries and their consequences. Since their conversion, the north and east galleries have been able to house exhibitions of all kinds, and they contain rooms of varying sizes which were built with this multiplicity of function in view. The transformation of the Grand Palais was influenced by the modern conception of the museum as a place for confrontations between the public and the creative mind rather than a sanctuary for select groups of experts; in addition to the exhibition rooms there are lecture rooms fitted with audiovisual equipment, closed-circuit television, a restaurant and rest-rooms. The first exhibition to

The porch and the east front of the Grand Palais

The glass dome in the hall of the Grand Palais

be held in the newly-renovated galleries was a massive Picasso retrospective in 1966, which attracted almost 850,000 visitors, and since then big exhibitions of the work of Léger and Matisse and an important exhibition of the work of French artists during the last ten years have proved the versatility of the Grand Palais. The new galleries have certainly been a success with the public: in the last four years, two and a half million people have visited exhibitions there.

At the beginning of this century, there were still only a few houses and gardens on the Champs-Élysées. Today this great avenue is the centre of a business district where most of the big Paris fashion houses have their headquarters.

The Paris haute couture industry is just over a century old. It was founded by an Englishman, Charles Frederick Worth, who opened a fashion house (which no longer exists today) on Rue de la Paix, which was then one of the boundaries of fashionable Paris. When the city expanded westwards towards Passy and Auteuil, the haute couture houses followed, and today they are established on both sides of the Champs-Élysées—on the Faubourg Saint-Honoré, Avenue Montaigne, Rue François Premier and Avenue George V. The hundreds of fashion journalists from all over the world who are privileged to know before the rest of the world what women will be wearing in six months' time flock to this small area of Paris at the end of January, when the summer collections are being shown, and at the end of July for the winter collections. The haute couture may have lost some of its power and mystique in recent years; in 1947 its authority and influence were absolute. When **Christian Dior** launched the New Look in that year, every woman in the Western world with any pretensions to elegance lowered her hemline by about seven inches. Since then, however, the fashion business has been revolutionized by the impact of a mass market of young people who have neither the desire nor the means to dress as their parents did. Attached to a traditional image of woman and priding themselves on the highest standards of craftsmanship, some of the grands couturiers have found it hard to keep up with the rapidly changing fashion scene, while some refuse to make any effort to do so. Others, however, have made their mark in the booming ready-to-wear business.

Members of the public can see the season's new outfits outside those times of the year when they are shown to the press and the big buyers, since the fashion houses generally employ their models all the year round and show their collections most afternoons. For those who do not want to buy a new dress this can be an opportunity to choose a perfume, scarf or tie bearing

Christian Dior, models
from the winter collection 1972-1973

the couturier's name. Some fashion houses make more money from accessories than they do from clothes.

The stretch of the Champs-Élysées between the Rond-Point and the Étoile is one of Paris's busiest and glossiest entertainment areas. Film premières are held here in cinemas which specialize in showing the latest releases, and as well as cabarets and nightclubs in the nearby streets, the Champs-Élysées is the home of the world-famous Lido revue, with its Amazonian **Bluebell Girls**, who are all at least five feet nine inches tall and who must include among their other qualifications "very strict moral principles."

The Bluebell Girls at the Lido

Military parade on the Champs-Élysées, July 14; foreground, the cadets of Saint-Cyr military academy

The Champs-Élysées at night

More than a mile long, the **Champs-Élysées** stretch between Place de la Concorde and the Étoile, and were originally laid out on the site of reclaimed marsh and market gardens by the seventeenth-century landscape gardener Le Nôtre. Unlike the higher section, the part which stretches from the Concorde to the Rond-Point is still lined with trees and gardens, as Le Nôtre intended. At first few people chose to live on the Champs-Élysées—there were still no more than six houses there at the beginning of the 19th century— but caterers set up their stalls beneath the shady trees; Ledoyen, which is today one of Paris's most famous restaurants, was already established there before the Revolution. The development of the avenue really began in the 19th century, with the building of the Arc de Triomphe, which was originally planned by Napoleon but took thirty years to build and was only completed during the reign of Louis-Philippe. Napoleon's remains were carried beneath the great arch on December 15, 1840, on the way to their final resting place in the Invalides, in the first of the great processions to pass down the Champs-Élysées. The victory parade of the allied troops after World War I was held here on July 14, 1919, and the following year the body of an unknown soldier was buried beneath the arch. The spot is marked by an eternal flame, and visiting heads of state always drive up the avenue to lay a wreath on the tomb.

In the 19th century, Victor Hugo could write of the Arc de Triomphe:

Thou whose curve from far away in the golden evening
Is filled with celestial blue, immense arch....

Not long ago, however, the clear expanse of sky framed by the archway was threatened by plans to build a tower block at La Défense which would have been visible from the Champs-Élysées and ruined the famous view. The public reaction was so hostile, however, that the plans will almost certainly be altered.

To celebrate France's national day, July 14 (which commemorates, not the fall of the Bastille in 1789, as is often thought, but the Festival of Federation which was held exactly a year later in honour of the newly promulgated constitution), a military parade passes down the Champs-Élysées, and each year the bright uniforms of the **cadets of Saint-Cyr military academy** stand out against the rather dull anonymity of most of the rest.

The Élysée Palace. Above: the entrance giving onto the Faubourg Saint-Honoré; below: the garden front

Just to the North of the Champs-Élysées runs the Faubourg Saint-Honoré, which was developed around the same time as the Faubourg Saint-Germain on the Left Bank. Several of the fine eighteenth-century houses have survived and are today embassies or clubs. The most magnificent of them is unquestionably the **Élysée Palace**, which was built in 1718 and has been the official residence of Presidents of the French Republic since 1873.

The **Faubourg Saint-Honoré** is the most elegant shopping street in Paris, with its booksellers, antique dealers and art galleries, and its renowned fashion and accessories shops. The luxury goods in the windows of houses like Hermès and Roger and Gallet are invariably presented in an attractive and original way, and in fact a competition for the best window display in the street is held each June.

Beyond the Faubourg Saint-Honoré to the North is a quiet and opulent residential area, the Monceau plain, whose atmosphere has changed little since the late 19th century, when Marcel Proust grew up there. Here as a young man he acquired and developed his taste for the fashionable world, whose powerful fascination he was unable to resist and whose vices he was to record with ferocious clarity. The district is crossed by a broad thoroughfare, Boulevard Haussmann, named after the man who rebuilt much of Paris during the reign of Napoleon III. Two of the big houses in the Monceau

The Faubourg Saint-Honoré from the shop window of Hermès

Maxim's

The commissionaire of Maxim's

plain district are museums open to the public. The Musée Jacquemart-André, which contains a collection of French, Dutch and Italian art, occupies a house built around 1870, and the Musée Nissim de Camondo, built somewhat later, is a museum of furniture and furnishings.

The area which lies between the Madeleine, the church of Saint-Philippe-du-Roule, Place de l'Alma and the Opéra, contains some of Paris's most outstanding restaurants as well as some of its most elegant shops. It goes without saying that the food in restaurants of this kind is excellent, and it takes a professional gourmet to recognize and appreciate the nuances of the great dishes and wines served in them. What distinguishes these top-class restaurants from one another is not so much their food as the kind of welcome they provide, their general atmosphere, and the kind of customer they attract. To take just one example, the reputation of **Maxim's** owes as much to its faithfully preserved 1900 decor and its history as it does to the quality of its food.

Founded in 1893, Maxim's quickly established a racy reputation as the boisterous meeting place of the wealthy and aristocratic international set of Europe. Edward VII of England, when he was Prince of Wales, Leopold II of Belgium, Russian Grand Dukes and the richest men in Paris were among the restaurant's regular customers, who dined in private rooms on the first floor or in the ground floor room with modern decorated panelling. As for the female customers of Maxim's, they belonged to the Paris demi-monde of the turn of the century which is so vividly described in the novels of Colette. No respectable society lady would have dared to show her face at Maxim's alongside such famous beauties as Liane de Pougy and Émilienne d'Alençon. Another Maxim's regular was the playwright Georges Feydeau, whose *The Lady from chez Maxim* gives an idea of the free and easy atmosphere which reigned in the restaurant during this period, when in order to avoid incidents women were only allowed in if they were accompanied. World War I dealt a death blow to the world which had brought Maxim's its fame and prosperity. Nevertheless, the restaurant has carefully preserved its decor and its tradition of hospitality, although its risqué reputation vanished long ago; today its many customers from all over the world eat in an atmosphere of unimpeachable respectability. Finally, Maxim's was the first restaurant in Paris to employ a pianist, and this tradition of entertaining the diners with background music has been maintained, although like any other top-class restaurant, Maxim's would not think of distracting its guests from the delights of conversation and gastronomy with a show. Maxim's stands on **Rue Royale,**

Jansen's boutique, Rue Royale

whose houses were built at the same time as Place de la Concorde and in similar style. Like the Faubourg Saint-Honoré, it is one of Paris's smartest shopping streets. Shops like Jansen's, the decorators who in 1971 created the setting for the 2,500th anniversary celebrations of the Persian Empire at Persepolis, bring to this part of central Paris a discreet atmosphere of luxury and prosperity. In fact Paris has always excelled in manufacturing luxury goods, and even in the 18th century the city was renowned for its fine embroidery, and the imagination, skill and resourcefulness of its craftsmen. A look in the windows of the great jewellers' shops in **Rue de la Paix** is enough to prove that this tradition has not died out.

Rue de la Paix and the Vendôme Column

Cartier the jeweller's, Rue de la Paix

The inventiveness of the jewellery design is very often as arresting as the quality of the precious stones themselves, and Parisians who never set foot in such shops are proud of them, nevertheless; like the great fashion houses, they embody a spirit of craftsmanship which is part of the Parisian heritage.

Avenue de l'Opéra and **Place de l'Opéra** were built during the Second Empire period, around the same time that architect Charles Garnier was building the Opéra itself, whose startling neobaroque façade so strikingly reflects the eclectic taste of the era. Work on the Opéra began in 1862, but by the time it was finished the Second Empire had fallen, a victim of the Franco-Prussian War. But even though it was inaugurated in 1875, under the Third Republic, it remains a fitting architectural symbol of the glittering and materialistic society of the France of Napoleon III. It is strange to think that while this building, with its profusion of styles and ornamentation, was under construction, Haussmann was ruthlessly ripping down historical buildings which had outlived their usefulness and tearing apart the old quarters of the city to make room for the wide roads which were so desperately needed. It is hard to see where the Opéra fits into this severe, utilitarian scheme of things. In fact it is the last example in Paris of a certain cluttered, fussy style of architecture lacking in grandeur and dignity. Only about twelve years after the Opéra was opened, work began on the Eiffel Tower, whose metal girders were to be left in complete structural bareness. Inside the Opéra, the labyrinth of corridors and lavish use of decoration reflect Garnier's conception of the use of space, which is completely at odds with modern ideas of what a theatre should be. (The auditorium can seat an audience of 2,158, and the stage can hold 450 performers.)

Garnier wanted to make the façade of the Opéra a work of art, and in fact there is one masterpiece among the sculptures which adorn it. This is the symbolic group by Carpeaux representing *The Dance*, which

The Opéra and the Café de la Paix

The Opéra: above, Chagall's ceiling; below, the great staircase

stands on the right of the façade at ground floor level. When Carpeaux's sculpture was first revealed to the public, there was an outcry; Parisians were scandalized by what they considered to be the lasciviousness of the dancers, although to modern eyes they are inoffensive in the extreme, the very epitome of health and gaiety. As for the Opéra's ballet company, its reputation too is healthy; each year it takes over the Opéra for the whole of the month of July.

Production costs and the costs of maintaining a rambling nineteenth-century building like the Opéra are enormous, and in spite of a government subsidy, the company faces many difficulties today. It is only on gala evenings that Garnier's masterpiece, the great staircase, appears in its true glory, when it is lined with the Republican Guards whose uniform is another survival from the Second Empire.

Some years ago traditionalists were shocked when André Malraux announced that he had given the painter Marc Chagall carte blanche to decorate the ceiling of the auditorium. However, when the paintings were finished, the critics were forced to admit that they did not jar with their surroundings and indeed added a touch of lightness to the heavy ornateness of the original decoration. Every age adds to and redecorates its public buildings, and now we must wait for posterity to judge whether or not **Chagall's ceiling at the Opéra** is a well-chosen example of twentieth-century art.

While the Opéra was being built, the first of a group of big department stores was taking shape in the nearby district. Today the department store is so familiar a part of the urban scene that it is hard to imagine the sensation caused when the Printemps store on Boulevard Haussmann first opened its doors in 1865. The Printemps was soon followed by others housed in groups of buildings in which metal was widely used. The **great staircase in the Galeries Lafayette**, one of Paris's biggest department stores, is reminiscent of its namesake in the Opéra, which was designed for the same purpose—to keep a big crowd moving freely.

Émile Zola's novel *Au Bonheur des Dames* (The Happiness of the Ladies) describes the despair of Paris's small shopkeepers as their customers deserted them for the new department stores, which offered a wider range of goods at more competitive prices than they could ever hope to do. However, the department store had come to stay. Even today, none of Paris's self-service shops is as big as the traditional department stores.

Stores like the Printemps and Galeries Lafayette pride themselves on the originality and attractiveness of their window displays, which are especially striking during the Christmas period, when spotlights play on clockwork toys miming La Fontaine's *Fables* and fantastic creatures from outer space. Some people believe that shopping centres are destined to be places where public meetings will be held and information exchanged; in other words that they will play the kind of role in our lives which cathedrals played in medieval society. It is up to the owners of the shops to take the initiative. A look at the **Christmas decorations on Boulevard Haussmann** suggests that this idea may not be so far-fetched after all. The decorations go far beyond the needs of advertising and attracting customers, as audiovisual shows and kinetic lighting create a setting in which people can enjoy themselves, forget the traffic which swirls past a few yards away, and recapture something of the atmosphere of a medieval fair.

Above: Christmas decorations, Boulevard Haussmann; below: the great staircase, Galeries Lafayette

7
PARIS AND ITS VILLAGES: FROM MONTMARTRE TO VINCENNES

The Butte Montmartre and the Sacré-Cœur

In 1860 a number of outlying villages such as Belleville, Montmartre, Auteuil and Passy officially became part of the city of Paris. Of these, Montmartre is the one which has most carefully preserved its rural character. This is partly because it is notoriously difficult to build on the Butte, the hill on which Montmartre stands. For centuries this was the site of a plaster quarry, and because the stone is crumbly and easy to dig, most of the houses are low and there are more gardens than in many other parts of Paris.

Although Montmartre existed as long ago as the Gallo-Roman period, it is only in relatively recent times that people settled there in any numbers. Until the Revolution, the Butte belonged to the Benedictine monastery whose little Romanesque chapel of Saint-Pierre can still be seen today, hidden away in the shadow of the great basilica of **the Sacré-Cœur**. Built after the Franco-Prussian War to plans by the architect Abadie, the Sacré-Cœur is a pastiche in Roman-Byzantine style inspired by the cathedral of Saint-Front in Périgueux in southwestern France. The stone, which came from quarries at Souppes, south of Paris, is still as dazzlingly white as it was when the church was first built, and strikes a harsh note among the prevailing Paris grey. From the terrace in front of the basilica there is a magnificent view over the city.

According to tradition, St. Denis, the first bishop of Paris, was martyred at the foot of the Butte Montmartre, whereupon he picked up his head and carried it a few miles away to the burial place he had chosen for himself and which has ever since been known as Saint-Denis. Because of this story

Montmartre: Place du Tertre

Montmartre : the vineyard

A picturesque figure of old Montmartre

people long thought that the name Montmartre came from the Latin "Mons Martyrum," but today scholars claim that a more likely origin is "Mons Mercurii," the hill of Mercury, to mark the site of a pagan temple some of whose pillars can still be seen in the church of Saint-Pierre mentioned above.

Life went on peacefully in medieval Montmartre under the jurisdiction of its Benedictine abbesses. People lived from working the plaster quarries, from market gardening, and from the mills which caught the north wind in their exposed position on the hill. By the 12th century, vines were being cultivated in Montmartre and the settlement was already connected by several roads to the growing city of Paris. By the 17th century, Parisians had country houses there, and in the 18th the village was particularly favoured by actresses.

We know what Montmartre looked like towards the end of the 18th century from the work of the French landscape painter Georges Michel, whose pictures depict stretches of chalky land with windmills silhouetted against stormy skies. Michel's vision of the Butte was essentially tragic, and as such quite out of keeping with what actually happened in Montmartre after the Revolution, when the abbey property was sold. The land was bought up by entrepreneurs, who built streets which they named after their wives—thus we have Rue Berthe and Rue Antoinette—and houses which attracted large numbers of artists. During the Romantic era, poets and musicians like Gérard de Nerval and Hector Berlioz helped to make Montmartre fashionable.

At the beginning of the 19th century there were still twenty-five mills on the Butte, and according to tradition the millers of Montmartre also kept bars where they sold *jinglet*, the blue and somewhat acid local wine which was by all accounts extremely drinkable. The only visible reminder of this period of Montmartre history is a small **vineyard** which has been replanted along Rue Saint-Vincent in memory of the original one, and a single mill which has survived as something more than the name of a café or nightclub. This is the "Blutefin," otherwise known as the Moulin de la Galette, which belonged for hundreds of years to the Debray family, one of whose members was killed by the Russians while defending the old wooden building during the invasion of March 1814. Ancient though it is, the mill does not go back to 1295, as tradition would have it, although some of its woodwork may date from the 17th century. It has been one of Paris's most popular dance halls ever since the late 19th century, when Renoir persuaded some of his friends to pose there for a picture which came to symbolize the Montmartre the Impressionists knew. Another painter who lived in Montmartre, Raoul

A Montmartre cabaret: the Lapin Agile, Rue des Saules

Dufy, once copied Renoir's *Moulin de la Galette* when he was alone and ill in the United States, as if the act of recreating the atmosphere of the Butte could somehow transport him back to his youth.

By the second half of the 19th century, Montmartre had acquired a reputation as the artists' quarter of Paris. Its night life was exciting, and many people came in search of entertainment to cabarets like the famous "Chat Noir" (whose poster by Steinlen can still be seen, along with other relics of old Montmartre, in the Musée du Vieux-Montmartre). Today the Chat Noir is only a memory, but another cabaret dating from the same period is still open. This is the **Lapin Agile**—the agile rabbit—whose sign shows a rabbit clutching a bottle and in process of escaping from a saucepan.

The stairs of Rue Foyatier

Houses in Rue Poulbot seen from Place du Calvaire

behind their gaiety. His vision of this show-business world was so powerful that its influence is still felt today: as we watch the performers in a variety show we look through eyes which have been conditioned by

Rue Foyatier

The Impressionists' favourite meeting place was Place Pigalle, at the foot of the hill, in the cafés where models could be hired. Manet, Degas and Pissarro did not seek inspiration for their work in Montmartre, in contrast with Renoir, who lived there at various times and painted several pictures in the village in addition to the *Moulin de la Galette*. During his Paris period, Van Gogh painted *La Guinguette* in the Bonne Franquette restaurant on the corner of Rue Saint-Rustique. However, the most passionate observer of Montmartre night life was Toulouse-Lautrec, who adopted the quarter as his home.

Toulouse-Lautrec's Montmartre paintings are realistically drawn caricatures of the inhabitants of Montmartre's night world of pleasure. His genius lay in his ability to understand the lives of those whose work is to organize other people's pleasure and his capacity for expressing the sadness that lies

Toulouse-Lautrec's graphic paintings.

Another artist who expressed the poetry of the **Montmartre landscape** was Maurice Utrillo. This painter *maudit* lived much of his life on the Butte and painted it many times. His work is suffused with a tragic view of the world which is a reflection of his own inner life rather than an objective view of Montmartre. For there is plenty of gaiety in Montmartre, which somehow manages to preserve its village charm, in spite of the crowds of visitors who each year take the funicular up the hill, or climb **the stairs of Rue Foyatier,** which runs beside it.

Scene from the revue "Zizi je t'aime," by Roland Petit at the Casino de Paris

Finally, no account of Montmartre could be complete without mentioning the decisive changes in the course of modern painting which took place there in the early years of this century, when Picasso lived and worked in the dilapidated old building on Place Émile-Goudeau known as the Bateau Lavoir—the laundry boat. Picasso went to live in the Bateau Lavoir as a young man of twenty-two in April 1904, and the five years he spent there span his Blue Period to the beginnings of Cubism. For Picasso and the group of artists and writers who were his friends, this was a period of acute poverty; one of them, the writer Max Jacob, wrote later that "we all lived poorly, but the amazing thing was that we managed to live at all." It was here that Picasso painted the *Demoiselles d'Avignon*, that seminal Cubist work.

But it is Montmartre's reputation as an entertainment district rather than its place in the history of art which makes it such a big tourist attraction. Along the boulevards at the foot of the hill are the cabarets and music-halls which have made the district famous throughout the world. The **Moulin Rouge** existed in Toulouse-Lautrec's day, and still stages the same kind of revue as it did around the turn of the century, with variety acts which can be easily followed by those who cannot speak or understand any French. Lower down the hill, at the **Casino de Paris**, Roland Petit and Zizi Jeanmaire have created a show in which one act contains an allusion to the exotic animal and jungle paintings of the Douanier Rousseau; it is an unexpected pleasure to find a reference to a work of art in a scene from a revue.

The boulevards which stretch between the church of the Madeleine and Place de la République, which were the gayest streets of nineteenth-century Paris, are still known as the "Grands Boulevards." Those around the Opéra are as lively as they were in their heyday.

The Moulin Rouge cinema and music-hall, Place Blanche

Shopping arcade: the Passage Jouffroy

Those around the Porte Saint-Martin and the Porte Saint-Denis, on the other hand, are no longer as fashionable as they were more than a century ago, when they were nicknamed "the boulevards of crime" on account of the melodramas which were the speciality of the numerous theatres in the district. Several of these theatres have survived, including the most famous of them all, the Theatre of the Porte Saint-Martin, whose great successes during the Romantic era included Victor Hugo's *Marion Delorme* and *Lucrecia Borgia*, and Alexandre Dumas's *Antony* and *La Tour de Nesle*. Edmond Rostand's perennially popular *Cyrano de Bergerac* also had its first performance at the Porte Saint-Martin in 1897.

On the Grands Boulevards today it is the cinemas which provide sensation-hungry audiences with the excitement which their nineteenth-century predecessors got from melodrama, although the so-called boulevard theatre of light comedy still has a faithful following.

The **Portes Saint-Denis and Saint-Martin** were built in 1672 and 1674 respectively in honour of Louis XIV's military successes. They were erected as an act of atonement by the city of Paris, which wanted the King to forget its rebellious behaviour during the Fronde, the period of unrest which marked the early years of Louis XIV's reign. Strangely enough, these monumental gates have never been properly integrated into their surroundings; they are too close to the undistinguished buildings of the nearby streets for their proportions to be fully appreciated. In fact it must be admitted that this area which was known as the "Faubourg of Glory" in the 17th century no longer really deserves the name. Nearby is the quarter of the Sentier, Paris's garment manufacturing area, whose **shopping arcades** still have the atmosphere of the second half of the 19th century. The expansion of the city towards the West has left this part of Paris a backwater, except for the main boulevards.

The Grands Boulevards: Porte Saint-Martin in foreground, with Porte Saint-Denis beyond

The Flea Market

The Flea Market

Turning back to the North we come eventually to the **Flea Market**, whose sprawling site lies just outside the Porte de Clignancourt. The Flea Market is something like a North African *souk*, a vast network of stalls set out in little alleys and streets, with the difference that only secondhand goods are on sale. Each of the stalls has its own special line to attract the crowds of aficionados who flock to the market on Saturdays and Sundays. (Fridays are reserved for antique-dealers.) The vendors cover a wide cross-section of humanity: some of them are one-time travelling salesmen who have always been in the secondhand trade; others are Paris antique dealers who use the Flea Market as an opportunity to get rid of their poorer-quality goods. The customers are equally various: they range from the legion of the curious on the lookout for nothing in particular, to collectors searching for the elusive piece which will complete their collection, and young married couples who are trying to furnish their homes cheaply. The Flea Market is a great place for bargaining and barter, and rumours about the objects for sale spread like wildfire. This grubby painting will probably turn out not to be a Delacroix... and this tattered drawing is certainly not a Dufy—it is a good idea not to set one's sights too high. You are less likely to be disappointed if you are looking for something like a stopper for a decanter, or perhaps an ornamental flask or a firescreen, or even the kind of thing which you would be unlikely to see elsewhere—a tapestry loom, for instance. Apart from its other delights,

The Flea Market

the Flea Market is one of the few places left in Paris where one can occasionally see little groups of three-card trick players trying to cheat some innocent bystander, keeping a weather eye open for the police at the same time.

The Canal Saint-Martin

The Canal Saint-Martin

Continuing our tour of the outer boulevards, we come to the canals around Porte de la Villette which were built by order of Napoleon when he was First Consul as a means of bringing water to Paris from the River Ourcq. By 1808, the basin of La Villette was receiving water brought as far as the Seine by the **Canal Saint-Martin** from the Ourcq and another river in the region, the Beuvronne. A contemporary writer was afraid that such abundant water might cause the Parisians to acquire and abuse the habit of bathing. He confessed that his main fear was that what he called an Asiatic luxury and what we would call a decent private water supply would cause Parisian morals to deteriorate.

Napoleon intended to buy up the land along the banks of the Canal Saint-Martin "so that fine houses can be built on both sides of it, and these can then be sold to the city of Paris." However, this plan was never put into effect, and the charm of the canal was only revealed to the French through Marcel Carné's two famous films, *Hôtel du Nord* and *Quai des Brumes*, which showed them the wide quays planted with trees and the nine locks which allow barges to make the eighty-foot drop between the basin of La Villette and the Seine. The extraordinary thing is that each of these films was made in a studio, in which the scenery around the canal was recreated. Nevertheless the atmosphere evoked in them was true to the life around the canal which **Balzac** once described as "a long white sheet framed by reddish stones and adorned with lime trees."

Rue de Belleville

Villa Olivier-Métra, in the Belleville district

The cemetery of Père-Lachaise was originally a garden created by Louis XIV's Jesuit confessor on land belonging to the Society of Jesus. At the beginning of the 19th century, when Napoleon decided to replace the church cemeteries of central Paris by four big "fields of rest" outside the city, the Père-Lachaise gardens were chosen as the site of one of them. Everything possible was done to make the gardens an attractive burial ground for the fashionable and the eminent. This tactic was successful; those who lie buried in Père-Lachaise range from Napoleon's Marshals to poets and novelists like de Musset and Balzac, historians like

Even today reminders of the countryside can be found in the circle of villages which were annexed by the city of Paris in 1860. In **Belleville**, Ménilmontant and Charonne there are still little streets of two- or three-story houses with their own gardens, just as there are in Montmartre. Visitors to Paris rarely think of exploring these quiet residential parts of the city, where many people live what amounts to a village life: they take the Métro to work, but apart from that they rarely emerge from their immediate neighbourhood and take little interest in what goes on in the city at large.

There are several beautiful parks and gardens in these

Chopin's tomb, Père-Lachaise cemetery

The Buttes-Chaumont gardens

Michelet, and musicians and painters like Chopin, Delacroix and Géricault. In Balzac's novel *Le Père Goriot*, the ambitious hero, Rastignac, stands at the top of the hill of Père-Lachaise and issues a challenge to the city he is determined to conquer. The most macabre associations of Père-Lachaise are connected with the Mur des Fédérés, the wall against which the last surviving resistance fighters of the Commune were shot by supporters of the legitimate French government in 1871; this is still a place of pilgrimage for left-wing militants. Opposite the entrance to the cemetery, Bartholomé's Monument to the Dead is a reminder that:

Sceptre and crown
Must tumble down,
And in the dust be equal made
With the poor crooked scythe and spade.

outlying quarters of Paris. Among them are the gardens of the **Buttes-Chaumont**, which were created by the man who reshaped Paris in the 19th century, Baron Haussmann, on hills which had been stripped of their trees and vegetation by the plaster of Paris quarrying. The lie of the land made it possible to create an English-style park, complete with artificial lake.

The parks and gardens of Paris provide a home for a remarkable number of species of birds. A researcher from the Paris Natural History Museum discovered that in addition to the sparrows, which were originally cliff birds and like living on tall buildings, there are sixty-eight pairs of owls in Paris, mainly living in cemeteries, where they are less disturbed than elsewhere. We shall soon be in a position to know whether Paris's new skyscrapers attract eagles, like those in New York.

None of Paris's medieval fortresses has survived, but just outside the city to the East stands the **Château de Vincennes**, which the great nineteenth-century historian Michelet called the Windsor Castle of the Valois family. Following a tradition started by the Capetian royal dynasty in the Middle Ages, French Kings visited Vincennes to hunt in the

The Château de Vincennes: the Sainte-Chapelle and the Queen's Pavilion seen from the keep

woods belonging to their crown lands, and according to a well-known story in French history, in the 13th century St. Louis dispensed justice beneath an oak tree in the forest. The present château dates back to the 14th century, when it was built by the monarchs of the dynasty which succeeded the Capetians, the Valois. It was the favourite residence of the Valois King Charles V, who was born there and built the great rectangular enceinte. He also finished the **keep** and began the **chapel**, which is similar in appearance to the Sainte-Chapelle, but in the flamboyant Gothic style. Its original Renaissance stained glass has been replaced.

Efforts are currently being made

to restore Vincennes to its original state as a royal palace, and to obliterate as far as possible all traces of the long period, which began in Napoleon's time, when it was used by the armed forces. On March 21, 1804, Vincennes was the scene of a crime which shocked Europe, the murder of the Duke of Enghien, on Napoleon's orders. During World War II, the German occupying forces blew up the casemates of the château and the King's pavilion before they left Vincennes on August 24, 1944. Paris itself did not burn, as Hitler had threatened, but Vincennes did. The cost of the admirably executed restoration work has been covered by war damages. The two pavilions dating from the youth of Louis XIV have been rebuilt, and the courtyard has been restored to its former position between the two porticoed galleries. The southern gallery, which was embedded in a casemate in 1840, was found almost intact after an explosion had destroyed the casemate itself.

The avenues through the Vincennes woods have been retraced so as to follow those of the 18th century. The military buildings scattered here and there are gradually disappearing, although new uses are being found for some of them. For example, the enormous sheds which formed part of the Vincennes munitions factory have been taken over by Ariane Mnouchkine's Théâtre du Soleil company, which is exploiting the empty buildings as an opportunity to get away from the traditional concept of the theatre, with its barrier between actors and audience, and creates novel settings designed to encourage the audience to become involved in the action. Here in deserted and apparently unpromising surroundings, an important experiment in collective theatre is going on.

The Château
de Vincennes: the keep

The floral gardens of the Bois de Vincennes

Vincennes zoo: the great rock

Polar bears in the Vincennes zoo

The other distractions of Vincennes include a racecourse, the gardens of the Tropical Centre, and the Zoological Gardens, which stretch over thirty-five acres. Created during the Paris Colonial Exhibition of 1931, the **Vincennes zoo** has since been considerably enlarged, and as far as possible the natural conditions of each animal's habitat have been recreated. Visitors can climb to the top of a 200-foot-high **rock** which is the home of the mountain goats and chamois. From the summit there is a magnificent view out over the surrounding woods, and looking in the direction of Paris one can see the big African Arts Museum Building which was also built for the 1931 Colonial Exhibition and which stands at the main entrance to the Vincennes woods. The collection housed in this museum completes the one in the Musée de l'Homme and covers those parts of the world which formed part of the French colonial empire in the 19th and the first half of the 20th century.

In 1969, an international flower show was held at Vincennes, and since then its site has been preserved as a huge **floral garden**.

The Vincennes woods are not as popular as their opposite number on the other side of the city, the Bois de Boulogne, and consequently they are wilder, more natural. However, frequent visitors to Vincennes feel that the woods are no longer as neglected as they once were, and fear that events like the Son et Lumière show in the château are opening the eyes of a wider public to the beauty of this unique fortress and its surroundings.

8

TOMORROW'S PARIS

The Eiffel Tower by night

When today's architects find themselves the object of sarcasm and ridicule, they should take heart from what late nineteenth-century wits said about the **Eiffel Tower** when it was erected on the Champ-de-Mars, near the classical buildings of the École Militaire. It was as controversial and as much criticized as the Montparnasse tower is today.

The "300-metre tower," as it was called by the man who built it, Gustave Eiffel, is actually 984 feet high and was erected for the 1889 Paris Universal Exhibition as a memorial to the French Revolution. "A great part of the civilized world will pass under this immense triumphal arch, symbolizing the peaceful victory of the human spirit," wrote Eiffel, who was already well known as an engineer for his use of iron girders. He wanted his tower "to represent for all time the art of the engineer and the century of industry and science." The construction work was soon finished. It took just over two years—from January 26, 1887 to March 31, 1889—to assemble the riveted metal beams which form both the skeleton and the body of the tower and which were prefabricated in a factory in the Paris suburb of Levallois-Perret. The tower's 12,000 parts were fitted into position by a work force which never amounted to more than 200 men. It was revolutionary for its day, and as it took shape, few people thought that it had any claims to beauty. However, Eiffel reminded his fellow architects, whose work was inhibited by excessive traditionalism, that the "first aesthetic principle of architecture is that the basic lines of a building should be determined by their suitability for its setting." Today the disapproval which was heaped on the Eiffel Tower has long been forgotten, and it has become the most famous and the most frequently visited landmark

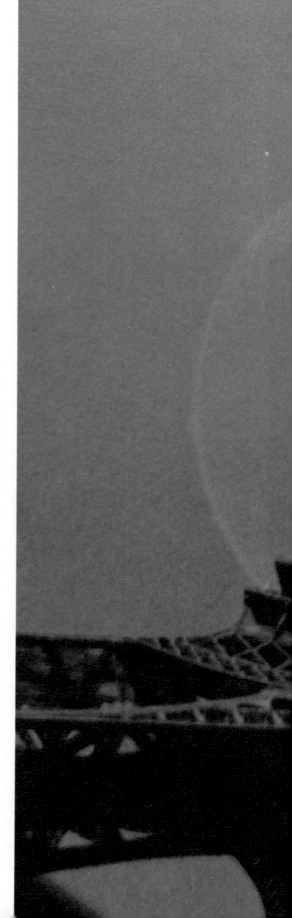

The Eiffel Tower

The shadow of the Eiffel Tower on the Pont d'Iéna and the gardens of the Palais de Chaillot

The gardens of the Champ-de-Mars
seen from the Eiffel Tower

in Paris. The main reason for its popularity is the panoramic view of Paris from its top platform. People say that on a clear day you can see for fifty miles in any direction, but the truth is that mist usually hangs over the hills which mark the rim of the basin in which Paris lies, lazily spread out around the meanders of the Seine.

Various international exhibitions like the one for which the **Eiffel Tower** was built have left Paris with a number of public buildings, each of which is in some way representative of the period in which it was built. One of these is the **Palais de Chaillot** which was built for the exhibition of 1937, across the river from the Eiffel Tower. The restrained and massive lines of the two curved buildings which form the Palais de Chaillot are representative of architectural fashions in the years immediately before the outbreak of World War II, in much the same way as the exposed ironwork of the Eiffel Tower is typical of design in the 1880s. There is an open space between the two wings of the Trocadéro, as the Palais de Chaillot is also called, and before it is a splendid view of the Seine, the Eiffel Tower, and the Champ-de-Mars gardens beyond. Inscriptions by the poet Paul Valéry are set in gold letters on the walls which flank the central area, providing a reminder that the Palace houses several museums: in the wing nearer to central Paris is the Musée des Monuments Français, which contains a collection of mural paintings and monumental sculpture, while the west wing is occupied by the Musée de la Marine and Paris's museum of ethnology and anthropology, the Musée de l'Homme. Beneath the central precinct which separates the two wings is a vast theatre. Its form is better suited to concerts than to plays, and it took all the fire and genius of the great French director Jean Vilar to attract the crowds in the early days of the state-subsidized Théâtre National Populaire, which has its headquarters there.

West of the Palais de Chaillot lies the expensive residential district of Passy and Auteuil, once villages and now part of Paris's 16th Arrondissement. Parisians who do not live in the 16th claim that they can recognize those who do from their slightly affected accents, and maintain that it is even possible to detect these real or imagined affectations of speech by listening to the waiters in the local restaurants, unless they are Spanish, as most of them are. There are still plenty of small detached houses and private gardens here, for the district kept much of its rural character up to the end of the last century. Although the house where Molière used to receive his friends has disappeared, Balzac's house in Rue Raynouard is still there,

Four bridges seen from the Eiffel Tower: the Pont Bir-Hakeim, the railway bridge, the Pont de Grenelle, the Pont Mirabeau

and has been converted into a charming little museum.

Unfortunately, the undisciplined private building that went on in Paris in the 19th century created some extremely ugly areas in the western parts of the city. Houses of all shapes and sizes were put up haphazardly, without any thought for unity of style or town planning. Though the house fronts in these parts of town are often imposing, their appearance is deceptive, for the staircases, courtyards and attics behind them are generally wretched. As for today's architects, posterity will find it hard to accuse them of lack of concern for town planning. They are aiming at nothing less than a complete reorganization of urban civilization, and one step in

Riverside development scheme in the 15th Arrondissement

this direction is to build upwards rather than outwards.

One Paris building in particular has had to face a storm of violent controversy, because of its situation on the edge of the old part of the city. This is the Montparnasse tower, which is the central feature of the development programme of the **Maine-Montparnasse quarter**. Its fifty-six floors are supported by a central core of concrete encased in a metal frame. The ground-plan is oval with a bite removed from each end in order to give a certain rhythm to what would otherwise be an expanse of bare wall. A wide range of amenities is being installed in the tower in an attempt to meet the spiritual and material needs of the thousands of people who will live and work in it.

Meanwhile a **riverside development scheme** is currently underway in the 15th Arrondissement, on a site more than half a mile long. It has been planned according to the principles of Le Corbusier: various activities are assigned to various levels of each building. For example, ground level is to be reserved for traffic, while two stories

The 7th Arrondissement and the Maine-Montparnasse quarter seen from the Eiffel Tower

The UNESCO building, Place Fontenoy

Vasarely's design for the front of the Radio Television Luxembourg building

up, a pedestrian precinct will give onto shops, hanging gardens and entrances to apartment blocks. Eighteen tower blocks are planned, with apartments in the upper stories and offices beneath.

It is not yet possible to form an opinion about the success or otherwise of these complexes, since none has yet been completed. However, one of their good points is that they give contemporary artists an opportunity to show what they can do. Promoters of new buildings are required by the French government to devote 1 percent of their total construction budget to decoration in the form of art. In this way a public art scaled to the needs of modern buildings is coming into being. Nevertheless, today's architecture, which has less than a century of tradition behind it, has not yet become a part of our way of life, and it is still suspect to those with conservative tastes. It is now heading for a period of classical balance, based on static geometrical masses which are in themselves austere and unappealing, and there is an urgent need for a new style of decoration to enliven this severity. In the case of the **UNESCO building**, the problem was solved by turning to well-known artists whose work had already been accepted by society at large. A fresco was commissioned from Picasso, a mobile from Calder, and a piece of sculpture from Henry Moore. There are also works by the French artist Bazaine and a Japanese garden designed by Nogachi in the UNESCO building, which was designed by three famous architects, Breuer, Nervi and Zehrfuss, in the form of a Y supported on pillars. The most attractive of all the works on display are **two ceramic walls by Miró**, even though they have been integrated into the plan of the building in a rather artificial way. The usual graphic elements one associates with Miró's work can be seen in the wall, whose effect is cheerful, optimistic. Today's art, like that of the Middle Ages, calls for international collaboration in every sphere.

The Op artist Victor Vasarely was commissioned to decorate the front of the **R.T.L. building**, the Paris headquarters of Radio Television Luxembourg, in Rue Bayard near the Champs-Élysées. His corrugated steel design has no structural connection with the architecture of the building, but it has all the characteristic hallmarks of Vasarely's work.

Television buildings play an important part in modern Paris architecture, befitting the importance of the medium itself, which has taken over from the book as the principal purveyor of contemporary culture. Art is beginning to benefit from the success of television, as architects and designers are being commissioned to construct buildings adapted to the special requirements of small-screen production.

Ceramic wall by Miró in the UNESCO building

The radio and television centre of the O.R.T.F., France's state-run broadcasting organization, was designed by the architect Henry Bernard. It is a good example of a functional building that is also visually appealing. There is a circular outer ring of buildings, nearly one-third of a mile in circumference, which is designed to provide acoustic protection for the recording studios which lie within it. Then there is an inner ring containing five theatres equipped for recording before live audiences, and twenty big studios. The lower stories of the inner ring, which has a circumference of 225 feet, are used for storing technical equipment, while the upper stories contain conference rooms and libraries of books and sound recordings. The sound and television archives are kept in the twenty-one stories of a central tower.

The Parc des Princes stadium

The idea behind all this seems logical enough: departments involving direct contact with the general public are situated in the outer ring, and the centre is reserved for technical operations. However, the results have not been entirely satisfactory, since the tower, which is acoustically almost independent of the rest of the building, is hardly used, and each day a large number of man-hours is lost by people caught up in the labyrinth of corridors connecting the offices with the studios. When French television did a programme on the world of Kafka in 1968, they were able to do the location shooting in their own building. But one thing that can be said for the O.R.T.F. building is that it is built on the scale of the problems that it has to solve.

The population of the Paris region rose steadily during the 1960s from 7½ million in 1962 to more than 8 million in 1968. The new **Parc des Princes** sports

The O.R.T.F. building

The Bois de Boulogne

The Hôtel Méridien-Paris, Boulevard Gouvion-Saint-Cyr

stadium is just one example of how the city is building new and bigger public amenities to satisfy this expanding population. The stadium has also, incidentally, provided France with a spectacular illustration of the gap that can develop between builders' original estimates and the final costs of construction.

The hotel industry is also trying hard to keep up with the demands of the growing tourist trade and the heavy influx of visitors to the big Paris trade fairs. A number of **new hotels** are being built on a lavish scale; most of them are in the western part of the city and most of them are in the international style favoured by big hotel chains from San Francisco to Tokyo. Their guests, who will travel more and more quickly as supersonic air travel causes the planet to shrink, will have to go out into the streets if they want to taste the atmosphere of Paris. One place they will surely visit is the **Bois de Boulogne**, a park stretching over 2,500 acres and incorporating artificial lakes, waterfalls, flower gardens, cafés, and two racecourses. Here rowing addicts can hire boats that date from the turn of the century, and art lovers can see the Bagatelle pavilion, a folly built for the Count of Artois in less than three months in 1775. Around it is a rose-garden laid out at the beginning of this century. The most modern museum in Paris, the Musée des Arts et Traditions Populaires, is also in the Bois de Boulogne, where it attracts visitors interested in French customs and folklore.

Meanwhile, at **La Défense**, across the Seine from the fashionable suburb of Neuilly, the Paris of tomorrow is taking shape. La Défense is a vast complex of office and apartment blocks, with transport facilities to serve them. It has been planned to house 50,000 office workers and 20,000 flat-dwellers, and to cater for the 70,000 vehicles that pass through every day. This traffic will go underground, beneath a concrete pedestrian precinct.

The Défense complex will eventually consist of twenty-one towers. They are all being built to the same groundplan, but the timelag between construction dates fortunately ensures that the decoration will be varied. Originally each one was to be 330 feet high, but so many businesses have decided to move their offices out from central Paris that the architects are already thinking in terms of heights of 500 or even 600 feet. One of the big projects at La Défense has already been completed—the CNIT (National Centre of Industries and Techniques) building, which consists of an enormous concrete roof rising fan-shaped from three supports. Two other buildings have been planned, but it is not yet certain that they will be built.

A rapid underground system already connects the new development to central Paris. This link is part of the R.E.R., the thirty-mile-long regional express Métro system, which will eventually reach out from the heart of Paris and join the eastern suburb of Boissy-Saint-Léger with Saint-Germain-en-Laye in the West. Three big stations in Paris are already in service: Nation, Étoile and **Auber**, near to Opéra; a fourth station is being built in Les Halles on the site of the recently-demolished market pavilions; here the express Métro system will connect with a north-south line. The new stations double up as shopping centres and meeting places, and are completely in tune with the idea of tomorrow's Paris of which La Défense is both the symbol and the incarnation.

The express Métro: Auber station

La Défense

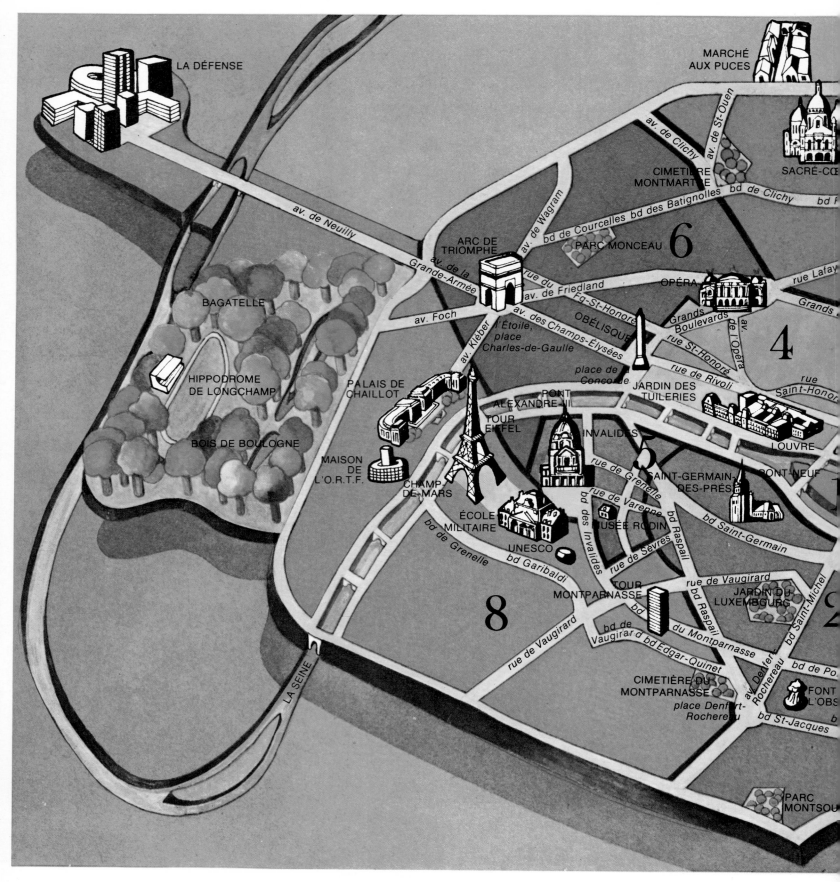

LA DÉFENSE

MARCHÉ AUX PUCES

av. de Clichy
av. de St-Ouen

CIMETIÈRE MONTMARTRE

SACRÉ-CŒ

av. de Neuilly

av. de Wagram

bd de Courcelles bd des Batignolles

bd de Clichy

bd F

ARC DE TRIOMPHE

PARC MONCEAU

6

rue Lafay

av. de la Grande-Armée

rue du

OPÉRA

av. de Friedland

Fg-St-Honoré

Grands Boulevards

rue de l'Opéra

Grands

4

BAGATELLE

av. Foch

av. Kléber

l'Étoile, place Charles-de-Gaulle

av. des Champs-Élysées

OBÉLISQUE

rue St-Honoré

rue de Rivoli

rue Saint-Honor

HIPPODROME DE LONGCHAMP

PALAIS DE CHAILLOT

place de Concorde

JARDIN DES TUILERIES

BOIS DE BOULOGNE

MAISON DE L'O.R.T.F.

TOUR EIFFEL

PONT ALEXANDRE-III

INVALIDES

LOUVRE

PONT-NEUF

1

CHAMP-DE-MARS

SAINT-GERMAIN-DES-PRÉS

3

ÉCOLE MILITAIRE

rue de Grenelle

rue de Varenne

bd Saint-Germain

UNESCO

MUSÉE RODIN

rue de Sèvres

bd des Invalides

bd Raspail

bd de Grenelle

bd Garibaldi

TOUR MONTPARNASSE

rue de Vaugirard

rue de Vaugirard

8

bd du Montparnasse

rue de Vaugirard

bd de Vaugirar

bd Edgar-Quinet

bd du Montparnasse

JARDIN DU LUXEMBOURG

bd Raspail

bd Saint-Michel

2

CIMETIÈRE DU MONTPARNASSE

place Denfert-Rochereau

av. Denfert-Rochereau

bd de Po

FONT L'OBS

bd St-Jacques

LA SEINE

PARC MONTSOU

APPENDICES

THE HISTORY OF PARIS

Lutetia, from its origins to the 10th century

In the middle of the 1st century B.C., the Roman conquerors of Gaul set up a garrison in a village on an island in the Seine and called it *Lutetia Parisiorum*. The Gallo-Roman town was connected to the river banks by two wooden bridges, and spread to the hillside which rose above the south bank, where an elegant quarter developed until it was destroyed by barbarian invaders at the end of the 3rd century A.D. The inhabitants of the settlement fell back onto the island which was beginning to be called Paris. In the 6th century Clovis, the first Merovingian King of Gaul, chose the city (which at that time covered less

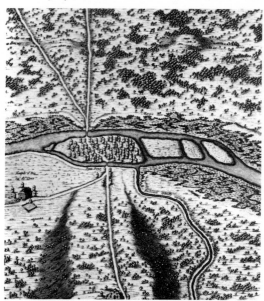

"Lutetia, or the first map of the city of Paris", by Nicolas de Fer (1728)

than twenty-five acres) as his capital. With the spread of Christianity, abbeys and chapels were built around the island which formed the city's nucleus, only to be ravaged by the Norman invaders in the 9th century. The city was triumphantly defended against the Normans in 886 by Bishop Gozlin and Eudes, Count of Paris, and became the capital of France at the end of the 10th century, with the accession of Hugh Capet, the founder of the Capetian dynasty of French Kings.

Paris, from the 10th century to the end of the 15th

Paris was largely rebuilt during the 11th and 12th centuries by the Capetians. The city wall begun by King Philip Augustus in 1190 surrounded an area of 1,100 acres, although it did not, strictly speaking, separate the country from the town, since there was still plenty of farmland within it. The wall, only a few traces of which survive today, on Rue Clovis, protected the city's commercial quarter on the northern bank of the Seine and the university on the southern bank. In the 14th century the wall was extended to include the villages which had developed outside it on the Left Bank. The Bastille fortress was one

The Palace and the Sainte-Chapelle, from "The Very Rich Hours of the Duc de Berry"

of the bastions of this new wall, which also contained within it the Louvre. Some of the public buildings which date from this period have survived, including Notre-Dame, the Sainte-Chapelle, the abbey church of Saint-Germain-des-Prés, the Hôtel de Sens and the Hôtel de Cluny.

From the Renaissance to the Revolution

Ruled by Kings who took a close interest in its development, during this period some of the city's finest public buildings were built, as well as its first planned squares and some its most important streets. From this time date the first stone bridges connecting the two banks of the Seine, Place des Vosges, Place Dauphine, Place Vendôme, Place des Victoires and Place de la Concorde; the domes of the Val de Grâce, the Invalides and the Panthéon;

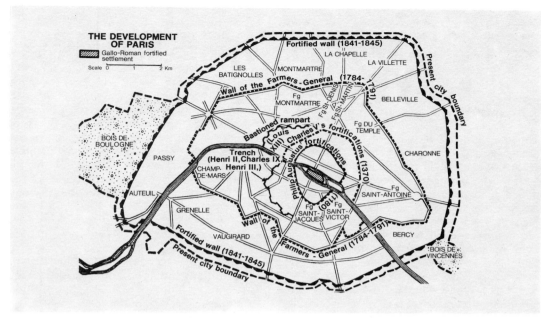

The development of Paris.
The city walls from
the Gallo-Roman period
to Thiers' fortifications

immense migration of workers, and tenement housing began to take the place of town houses and villas surrounded by gardens. In 1840 the Prime Minister of the day, Adolphe Thiers, ordered work to begin on the fortified wall which was later to play a key role during the siege of Paris in 1870. This "enceinte de Thiers," as it was known, ran around the suburban communities which stood outside the Wall of the Farmers General and which became part of the city in 1860. The Opera, the Eiffel Tower, the metal bridges across the Seine, the stations, and the first stages of the Métro all date from the 19th century, when the city was also provided with drinking water and its network of sewers.

Paris today and tomorrow

The only way to find vacant land in Paris today is by demolishing existing buildings

the colonnade façade of the Louvre, the Champs-Élysées and the École Militaire. Private houses were now built in durable materials and consequently a large number of them have survived—seventeenth-century houses in the Marais district, eighteenth-century ones in the Faubourg Saint-Germain and the Faubourg Saint-Honoré. After 1680, French Kings lived outside the city at Versailles, but their ministers continued to preside over the city's development: fine new squares were built, Paris became a centre of luxury industries and a city much visited by tourists. In 1785, the Wall of the Farmers General, which was not a fortification but simply a wall marking the city's fiscal boundaries, included almost all the faubourgs, or suburbs, which had lain outside previous walls and had by now been the site of extensive building.

The 19th century

Although Napoleon did not have the time to bring all his plans for Paris to fruition, he left his mark on the city in the church of the Madeleine, the Vendôme column, Rue de Rivoli, the Arc de Triomphe which stands at the top of the Champs-Élysées and its smaller counterpart on Place du Carrousel. However, the real creator of modern Paris was Baron Haussmann, Prefect of the Seine between 1853 and 1870, who demolished many of the city's old buildings and drove new streets through

Riverside development in the 15th Arrondissement   Development programme for the Défense quarter

the dense labyrinth of the medieval city. Among Haussmann's achievements are Avenue de l'Opéra, Boulevard Saint-Germain, and a North-South axis running from the Gare de l'Est to the Observatory. He also built a network of avenues around new squares in the popular eastern quarters of the city. These were built partly for strategic reasons; an outbreak of revolution could be more easily suppressed on broad boulevards than in the warren of narrow streets which they replaced. Meanwhile, the Industrial Revolution had attracted an

which are no longer suitable for modern needs. There has been extensive building development in what were until very recently the poorer parts of the city, and large numbers of high-rise buildings have gone up in the dormitory suburbs. Today the city of Paris is the centre of a whole developing region, and no longer simply an entity in itself. Each year the conurbation spreads further into the surrounding countryside, while less and less people live in the centre of the city, where they spend much of their work and leisure time.

HOTELS

Paris has a range of hotels to suit every taste and budget, from those of luxury class to small family hotels providing simply a room and breakfast. It is always advisable to book in advance, especially during holiday periods, but those who find themselves in Paris without accommodation should contact an official organization, the Accueil de France, which is just off the Champs-Élysées at 7 Rue Balzac, 8ᵉ (Tel. 359 52 78 and 359 48 00). Open every day from 9 a.m. until midnight, the Accueil de France provides information and help to visitors looking for hotel rooms.

Among the city's great hotels of international class are the Ritz (15 Place Vendôme), the Plaza-Athénée (23-27 Avenue Montaigne), the George V (29-31 Avenue George-V), the Bristol (112 Rue du Faubourg-Saint-Honoré), and the Intercontinental (3 Rue de Castiglione). All these hotels are on the Right Bank. The biggest hotel on the Left Bank is the Lutétia, 43 Boulevard Raspail, which is favoured by provincial Senators and Deputies. The Paris Hilton is at 18 Avenue de Suffren.

L'Hôtel, at 13 Rue des Beaux-Arts, was originally the Hôtel d'Alsace, where Oscar Wilde died in 1900. It has been transformed into what must be one of the most picturesque (and expensive) small hotels in the world; each room has been furnished individually with period furniture and velvet wall covering. Also on the Left Bank, also small (twenty-five rooms), is the Relais Bisson, 37 Quai des Grands-Augustins, where guests can choose between a fine view overlooking the Seine or a quieter room giving onto the courtyard.

A small, elegant hotel on the Right Bank is the Hôtel Bellman, 37 Rue François-Iᵉʳ; the bar is frequented by journalists from *Paris-Match* higher up the street. A charming little Left-Bank hotel giving on to a little garden is the Hôtel des Marronniers, 21 Rue Jacob.

GETTING AROUND IN PARIS

The only way to be sure of reaching your destination quickly is to take the Métro (full title: *chemin de fer métropolitain*), which runs underground most of the time, but occasionally emerges—at Bastille station, for example, in Montmartre, and for part of the distance between Passy and Montparnasse. Outside rush hours, travelling conditions on the Métro are fairly comfortable. Some stations, like the Louvre and Franklin-D.-Roosevelt, have been specially decorated, while Denfert-Rochereau station is sometimes used for exhibitions of work by young artists. The big new stations on the regional express Métro—Auber, Nation, and Étoile—are particularly impressive.

Paris has traffic problems, and for this very reason the bus is an ideal way to see the city—as long as you have plenty of time at your disposal. Métro tickets are valid on Paris buses; they can be bought individually or in books of ten at Métro stations and authorized shops (the address of the nearest point of sale is attached to bus stops). Bus drivers sell individual tickets. Each bus route is divided into sections (see map on each bus stop and inside the bus); one ticket is valid for up to two sections, over two sections you need two. The Paris city transport authority, the Régie Autonome des Transports Parisiens (usually abbreviated to RATP), also issues a special weekly runabout ticket for tourists. For further information, contact the RATP, 53 bis Quai des Grands-Augustins; tel. 346.42.03.

Pleasure boats on the Seine sail from the Eiffel Tower, the Pont de l'Alma and the Pont-Neuf. This is a pleasant and entertaining way of seeing Paris by day or by night.

There are plenty of taxi ranks in Paris, but it is often worthwhile phoning one of the companies linked to their taxis by short-wave radio. An important thing to remember is that taxis showing the two small lights beside their "taxi" sign are not for hire.

PARIS MUSEUMS

There are many museums in and near Paris. Since they are not controlled by a single authority, their opening hours and entrance fees vary. However, most museums are closed on Tuesdays. Many of the big Paris museums have more than one speciality and contain objects from various periods.

Antiquity and early Middle Ages

- Musée de l'Homme, Place du Trocadéro, Paris 16ᵉ: Prehistory.
- Musée du Louvre, Palais du Louvre, 1ᵉʳ: Department of Oriental antiquities, Egyptian antiquities, Greek and Roman antiquities.
- Musée de Cluny, 6 Place Paul-Painlevé, 5ᵉ: Gallo-Roman baths and objects excavated in the Paris region.
- Cabinet des Médailles, Bibliothèque Nationale, 56 Rue de Richelieu, 2ᵉ: Classical antiquity, medieval gold, silver and jewellery.
- Musée des Antiquités Nationales, Château de Saint-Germain-en-Laye (Yvelines): Prehistory and Gallic civilization down to the Merovingian period.

The Middle Ages and the Renaissance

- The Louvre: Departments of painting, French sculpture, furniture and objects.
- Musée de Cluny: Medieval objects and works of art.
- Musée des Monuments Français, Palais du Trocadéro, 16ᵉ: Mouldings and reconstructions of frescoes from buildings all over France.

17th and 18th century

- The Louvre: The same departments as for the previous period.
- Musée des Arts Décoratifs, 107, Rue de Rivoli, Paris 1ᵉʳ: Furniture and objects, down to the present day.
- Musée Carnavalet, 23 Rue de Sévigné, 3ᵉ: History of Paris; classical furniture and furnishings.
- Musée du Petit Palais, Avenue Churchill, 8ᵉ: Decorative arts; nineteenth- and early twentieth-century French art.
- Musée Jacquemart-André, 158 Boulevard Haussmann, 8ᵉ: A private collection of paintings, objects and furniture, from the Renaissance to the 18th century.
- Musée Nissim-de-Camondo, 63 Rue de Monceau, 8ᵉ: A private collection of eighteenth-century furniture and objects.

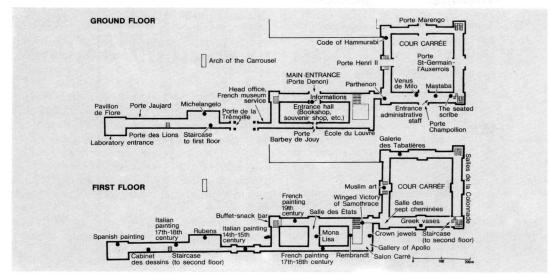

GROUND FLOOR

Porte Marengo
Code of Hammurabi
COUR CARRÉE
Arch of the Carrousel
Porte Henri II · Porte St-Germain-l'Auxerrois
MAIN ENTRANCE (Porte Denon) · Parthenon · Venus de Milo · Mastaba
Head office, French museum service
Informations
Pavillon de Flore · Porte Jaujard · Michelangelo
Porte de la Trémoille
Entrance hall (Bookshop, souvenir shop, etc.)
Entrance administrative staff · The seated scribe
Porte des Lions · Staircase to first floor
Porte Barbey de Jouy · École du Louvre · Porte Champollion
Laboratory entrance
Galerie des Tabatières
Salles de la Colonnade

FIRST FLOOR

Muslim art · COUR CARRÉE
French painting 19th century · Winged Victory of Samothrace · Salle des sept cheminées
Buffet-snack bar · Salle des États
Italian painting 17th-18th century · Rubens · Italian painting 14th-15th century
Greek vases
Spanish painting · Mona Lisa · Crown jewels · Staircase (to second floor)
Cabinet des dessins (to second floor) · Staircase · French painting 17th-18th century · Rembrandt · Gallery of Apollo · Salon Carré
0   100   200 m

The Louvre

The 19th century

- The Louvre: The same departments as for the previous period.
- Musée du Jeu de Paume, Place de la Concorde, 1er.
- Musée de l'Orangerie, Place de la Concorde: Monet's *Nymphéas*.
- Musée Marmottan, 2 Rue Louis-Boilly, 16e: French Empire furniture and furnishings and a collection of paintings by Monet and other Impressionists left to the museum by Monet's son, Michel.
- Musée Eugène-Delacroix, 6 Rue Furstenberg, 6e. House where the painter lived.
- Victor Hugo's house, 6 Place des Vosges, 4e.
- Rodin Museum, 77 Rue de Varenne, 7e.
- Balzac's house, 47 Rue Raynouard, 16e.
- Musée Gustave-Moreau, 14 Rue La Rochefoucauld, 9e: The works of the great painter and engraver who was also the teacher of Rouault.

Modern Art

- National Museum of Modern Art, 13 Avenue du Président-Wilson, 16e, and, in the opposite wing of the same building, (number 11), the Modern Art Museum of the City of Paris.
- Centre National d'Art Contemporain, 11 Rue Berryer, 8e: Collects information on all aspects of contemporary art and holds exhibitions.
- The Grand Palais, (Avenue de Selves, 8e), the Musée des Arts Décoratifs (107 Rue de Rivoli, 1er) and the Musée Galliera (10 Avenue Pierre-Ier-de-Serbie, 16e) often hold temporary exhibitions of the work of contemporary artists.

Specialist museums

French ethnography:
- Musée des Arts et Traditions Populaires, Route de Madrid, 16e: A collection dealing with life in the French countryside, housed in a modern building.

World ethnography:
- Musée de l'Homme, Place du Trocadéro, 16e: Man's origins and activities.
- Musée Guimet, 6 Place d'Iéna, 16e: Asiatic arts.
- Musée Cernuschi, 7 Avenue Velasquez, 8e: Chinese art.
- Musée des Arts Africains et Océaniens, 293 Avenue Daumesnil, 12e.

Scientific museums:
- Musée National des Techniques, Conservatoire des Arts et Métiers, 292 Rue Saint-Martin, 3e: In the buildings of the former abbey of Saint-Martin-des-Champs.
- Palais de la Découverte, Grand Palais, Avenue Franklin-D.-Roosevelt, 8e.
- Muséum National d'Histoire Naturelle, 57 Rue Cuvier, 5e.
- Musée de la Chasse et de la Nature, Hôtel Guénégaud, 60 Rue des Archives, 3e.

Historical museums:
- Musée de l'Histoire de France, Archives Nationales, Hôtel de Soubise, 60 Rue des Francs-Bourgeois, 3e.
- Musée de l'Armée, Hôtel des Invalides, 7e.
- Musée de la Légion d'Honneur, Hôtel de Salm, 2 Rue de Bellechasse, 7e.
- Musée des Gobelins, 42 Avenue des Gobelins, 13e: The museum is housed in the tapestry manufactory founded by Louis XIV; it is possible to visit a tapestry museum and the workshops where tapestries are still woven today.

SHOPPING

The Paris luxury trade is still concentrated in one or two districts in the centre of the city, where elegant shops still manage to survive competition from the big department stores. The most interesting streets for window shopping are: the Faubourg Saint-Honoré, Rue Royale and the Champs-Élysées on the Right Bank; and on the Left Bank, Boulevard Saint-Germain (between Boulevard Saint-Michel and Rue du Bac), Rue de Rennes between Rue du Four and Place Saint-Germain-des-Prés, and Rue Jacob.

Antique shops, art galleries and bookshops

The Saint-Germain-des-Prés district—Rue Bonaparte, Rue des Saints-Pères, Rue Jacob, Rue de Grenelle and Rue de Varenne—contains shops and galleries dealing in antique furniture, rare books, curios, modern painting and design.

Around Paris's central salesrooms, the Hôtel Drouot, are shops dealing in antique furniture, engravings and books. These are mainly concentrated on Rue Drouot, Rue de Châteaudun and Rue La Fayette.

There are a number of art galleries (modern painting and old masters), bookshops, antique shops and decoration shops between the Madeleine and the Arc de Triomphe; the main centres are the Faubourg Saint-Honoré, Rue La Boétie, Boulevard Haussmann and Avenue Matignon.

The Flea Market, at Porte de Clignancourt.

Fashion

There are several haute couture houses around Place Vendôme; most of the others are between Place Beauvau and Place de l'Alma.

Many avant-garde fashion shops are to be found in the Saint-Germain-des-Prés quarter on and around Rue de Sèvres.

More traditional clothes are to be found near the big department stores near the Opéra, and especially in Rue Tronchet and around the Madeleine.

Jewellery

For traditional jewellery: Place Vendôme and Rue de la Paix.

Costume jewellery: Rue de Rivoli and the Saint-Germain-des-Prés district, where there are also several shops specializing in ancient jewellery. Modern jewellery can often be found on pavement stalls.

PARISIANS LOOK AT PARIS

Jean Dutourd *is a well-known French novelist and essayist who was born in Paris and has set some of his best-known novels there. For seven years he was the theatre critic of the Paris evening paper "France-Soir."*

Entertainment

"The first thing the prospective theatre-goer in Paris should do is buy a little magazine called *Pariscope* which is on sale on all the newsstands and appears on Wednesdays. It contains theatre addresses and telephone numbers, curtain up times, and a mine of other useful information about the week's entertainment in Paris. Read it and you will find that there are somewhere in the region of 100 theatres in Paris, not counting café-theatres and cabarets.

An evening at the Comédie-Française is a must. This beautiful theatre is the headquarters of one of the few companies in the world where star actors can be found playing small parts. The French classics are the mainstay of the Comédie-Française's repertory. The company occasionally presents Molière adapted to suit modern taste, sometimes with unfortunate results; however, it is always incomparable in Marivaux, Labiche, Musset, Montherlant, and so on.

With its grandiose proportions, extravagant gilt and marble decoration, and ceiling by Chagall, the Opéra building is a show in itself.

In a way, theatres are like great restaurants whose reputation disappears with the departure of the chef. Thus the Athénée theatre lost a part of its soul with the death of its guiding spirit, Louis Jouvet, as did the Théâtre National Populaire (usually known by its initials as the TNP), when its founder, Jean Vilar, died not long ago. An exception to this general rule is the Atelier theatre, where André Barsacq has managed to impose his own personality and at the same time keep alive some of the spirit of the great Charles Dullin.

The so-called Boulevard theatre specializes in light comedy played by actors with the particular skills and timing which this form of drama requires. The reputations of some of the many theatres which present light comedy go back to the turn of the century or the Twenties. They include: the Palais-Royal, the Bouffes, the Gymnase, the Michodière, the Variétés, and the Madeleine. Another famous theatre of this kind, the Comédie des Champs-Élysées, has mainly produced plays by Jean Anouilh during the last few years.

The tiny Théâtre de la Huchette occupies a curious place on the Paris theatre scene. For the past sixteen years, the same two plays by Eugène Ionesco have been performed there.

Several Paris theatre companies choose to work in unusual places. The Renaud-Barrault company (run by the distinguished actor-director Jean-Louis Barrault and his wife Madeleine Renaud) has acted Claudel in the largely-disused Gare d'Orsay, and Ariane Mnouchkine's Théâtre du Soleil company puts on performances in a munitions factory out at Vincennes.

Operettas can be seen at the Châtelet and Mogador theatres, and sometimes at the immense Théâtre de Paris, which has been known to put on lavish productions of Offenbach.

In spite of the competition of cinema and television, Paris theatre is intensely active. Whether he is entertained by a play or bored by it, the Paris theatregoer cannot fail to be struck by the passion and skill with which it has been presented." J.D.

Further information :

Live entertainment in Paris is currently going through a period of crisis and rethinking caused largely by the popularity of television and the cinema. Nevertheless, the city offers an enormous range of live entertainment:

The state-subsidized theatres regularly put on new plays in addition to the mainstays of the classical repertory. Each season the leading Paris subsidized theatres

—the Comédie-Française, the Odéon, the Théâtre National Populaire at the Palais de Chaillot, the Théâtre de la Ville (in a modernized theatre on Place du Châtelet), and the Théâtre de l'Est Parisien—stage new productions.

Music and dance. Apart from occasional performances elsewhere (most of them at the Théâtre des Champs-Élysées, which plays host to an international dance festival each autumn), the Opéra is the only place in Paris where ballet is regularly performed. Each week there is at least one performance, and throughout July the Opéra is entirely given over to ballet. The Paris concert programme is rich and varied : international stars give recitals in concert halls like the Salle Pleyel near the Champs-Élysées, and chamber music can be heard in a wide variety of settings—from the city's churches to the University Law Faculty and the Conservatoire, while concerts are regularly held at the headquarters of the state broadcasting system, the O.R.T.F.

There are frequent productions of musical comedies and operettas, especially at the Châtelet and Mogador theatres, and shows imported from the United States are sometimes staged in Paris vaudeville theatres, with varying success.

The Boulevard theatre still has its devotees among those who appreciate its particular brand of entertainment uncomplicated by philosophical or political messages. New productions usually come on during the autumn, at the time of the Paris motor show, which traditionally attracts crowds of visitors who enjoy this type of play.

Avant-garde theatre companies often choose to work in unlikely places like the Vincennes munitions factory where Ariane Mnouchkine's Théâtre du Soleil troupe has put on its interpretations of the French Revolution, *1789* and *1793*. Other places where avant-garde theatre companies have worked in the last year or two include the Espace Cardin, on the Champs-Élysées, and the wrestling hall in Montmartre where Jean-Louis Barrault's troupe put on their show *Rabelais*.

Music-halls and cabarets present a whole range of shows from lavishly produced revues with scantily dressed dancers (the Lido, the Casino de Paris, the Folies Bergères) to one-man shows. Cabaret shows in Montmartre and around the Opéra are often staged in restaurants—where the diners sometimes find themselves taking part in the entertainment.

Singing stars appear in theatres and music-halls like the Olympia, sometimes alone, sometimes as the star of a cabaret.

As far as cabarets are concerned, the tone tends to be traditional in Montmartre, more way-out in Saint-Germain-des-Prés. Finally, many restaurants have their own musicians and singers to entertain their customers.

Cinemas showing the latest films are almost all to be found either on or near the Champs-Élysées or on and around the Grands Boulevards between the Madeleine and Richelieu-Drouot. Especially in the Latin Quarter there are many small cinemas which specialize in showing old films and experimental new ones aimed at a limited audience. Lastly, there are the two cinemas of the Cinémathèque Française, one in the Palais de Chaillot, the other in Rue d'Ulm, which each day present five or six films from their archives, which contain an unrivalled record of the art of cinema throughout the world.

Count Christian de Fels *was born in 1919 and grew up in a family where the great French culinary traditions were zealously upheld. Passionately interested in food, he is a member of the exclusive French gastronomic society, the "Club des Cent." With another French gastronomic journalist, Pierre Marchant, he contributes a weekly column to the French business magazine "Entreprise."*

Restaurants

"Paris has a strong claim to be the gastronomic capital of the world, and the city offers such an abundant choice of restaurants that it would be difficult, in the course of a single lifetime, to get to know them all.

Some have a worldwide reputation ; others, less well known, provide good food and a welcoming atmosphere, and keep alive the tradition of the bistro.

As far as the former are concerned, the prize must go to Maxim's, which has been attracting people from all over the world for well over half a century. The welcome from the maître d'hôtel, Roger—the successor of the famous Albert—is agreeable and the food is excellent. Crayfish in aspic followed by ribs of beef with pommes Maxim's (a scalloped potato cake), only gives a slight indication of the chef's capabilities. The cellar is beyond praise.

The Tour d'Argent, with its magnificent view out over the Seine, specializes in duck dishes. Particularly delicious is the

149

soft and moist duck with four peppers. The cellar contains many remarkable wines.

Lasserre is another of Paris's great restaurants. Its opening roof makes it a particularly cool and pleasant place to eat during the summer. The fillet of brill with sorrel is remarkable, and the wine list is first-rate.

These restaurants are expensive, but for those whose budget is more limited, there are many restaurants in Paris where it is possible to eat well for a reasonable price.

If you decide to lunch at Madame Cartet's restaurant (called simply Chez Cartet), at 62 Rue de Malte, you will find the atmosphere of provincial France and good bourgeois cuisine. If you like garlic, you cannot go wrong if you try her brandade de morue (pounded cod), while the duck with figs, from a recipe by the great French philosopher of the kitchen Brillat-Savarin, is particularly fine. For dessert, try the delicious apple tart which is one of Madame Cartet's specialities.

Les Belles Gourmandes, at 5 Rue Paul-Louis-Courier in the 7th Arrondissement, is also recommended. One of the young chef's specialities is fillet of duck cooked pink, and the cellar contains, among other wines, an impeccable Médoc, a Lynch-Bages 1964.

An excellent fish restaurant is La Marée, 1 Rue Daru (8e), where they serve a remarkable sole garnished with diced lobster.

Those who want to reconcile good eating with a strictly limited budget should try Aux Crus de Bourgogne, 3 Rue Bachaumont (2e), which is kept by a real old-style bistrot "patronne." The foie gras is astonishingly cheap, and the crayfish is first class; wash it down with an unpretentious Corsican wine. The atmosphere in this restaurant is particularly pleasant.

La Petite Tour, 11 Rue de la Tour (16e) is equally pleasant and informal. Among its specialities are a pancake containing ham, lobster grilled with herbs, and veal kidneys cooked with mustard. The price is reasonable and the welcome is warm.

Finally, on the other side of town at 22 Place Denfert-Rochereau is La Chaumière des Gourmets, where you can start with a succulent fish stew, Dieppe-style. This can be followed by a duck with green pepper à la Ranavallo, the like of which I have never tasted elsewhere. The selection of cheeses includes one original touch—a goat's cheese doused in olive oil with herbs."   C. F.

Further information :

The quality of Paris restaurants is a by-word. Apart from the truly great restaurants, most of which are to be found in the centre of the city, Paris is rich in places offering good food at reasonable prices. In fact outside the great restaurants, price differences between one restaurant and another often depend largely on factors such as service and general ambience rather than any striking variations in the quality of the food itself. Scattered through the city there are also plenty of restaurants serving non-French cuisine—Chinese, Greek, Italian and Russian—although most of these speciality restaurants are concentrated in the Latin Quarter. But those whose gastronomic aim while in Paris is to eat French food will find an abundance of bistros offering traditional regional dishes.

For twenty-five years gallery-owner Denise René *has been in the forefront of one of the liveliest movements on the French art scene. She opened her first gallery in 1945 and since then has played a big role in promoting the work of Vasarely, Arp, Mortensen, Herbin and many other contemporary artists. Museums and art galleries all over the world contain works by these painters and sculptors who have affected our whole environment through their influence on fashion and advertising.*

Art galleries

"My meeting with Vasarely at the Café de Flore in Saint-Germain-des-Prés in 1945 and his suggestion that I should convert part of my apartment into a picture gallery were the starting points of an adventure which has now lasted for twenty-seven years. During this time I have helped people to get to know and love the form of art known as abstract constructive art, which is a combination of intelligence and harmony and which derives its nobility from the geometric balance with which it is created.

I cannot remember whether I realized at the time of my first exhibition, which was devoted to the work of Vasarely, that I was creating a meeting place and a link for these artists who, with their very different outlooks, were working within a form of artistic expression which lay outside what was accepted at that time.

After the upheavals of the war, artistic taste seemed to be lacking in self-renewal. Paris was cut off from the influence of the great creative artists then working outside France. As I came to know these artists, I began to feel that here was the renewal of a taut, dynamic art totally opposed to the destructive impulse. I experienced this with a feeling of shock one day at an exhibition of work by Atlan. Five unknown artists left their canvases with me; they were Dewasne, Deyrolle, Hartung, Marie Raymond and Schneider. Standing before their austere, well-constructed works, I understood immediately the direction I would take, in spite of the difficulties I could see looming up.

To keep a gallery like mine is rather like training and managing a team. To ensure our survival, I organized prestige exhibitions like "150 Picasso drawings" and "From Ingres to our times". But I also organized a large number of avant-garde exhibitions, which provided an occasion for meetings where people like the museum curator Jean Cassou, the composer Pierre Boulez, and men of letters like Marcel Brion were given a hearing. In this way the work of unknown and little-known artists was presented to the public, which I am afraid showed a fairly consistent indifference to it. These were abstract painters, geometrically inclined, who owed much to Mondrian and Herbin.

In 1955, when public taste was moving towards abstract expressionism and tachism, I made room in my "Mouvement" exhibition for artists like Vasarely, Agam, Buri, Calder, Duchamp, Soto and Tinguely, who were introducing the idea of time and duration into art. They were trying to increase the number of effects created by a work of art (its appearance might change as the spectator changed position, it might be mobile sculpture producing a large number of light effects), so that it could be approached not at a single moment in time, as is the case with classical art, but during a certain length of time. This historic exhibition of what became known as "kinetic art" had a great success because of its curiosity value, and its effects spread through Italy, Germany, Switzerland, Yugoslavia and the Scandinavian countries. Around the same time, the Paris Museum of Modern Art was showing work by the G.R.A.V. (Groupe de Recherche d'Art Visuel), in which people like Le Parc, Morellet, Garcia Rossi, Sobrino, Stein and Yvaral were trying through their art to transform the relationship between artists and the public. For evidence of the impact of these movements on modern life we need look no further than the clothes designed by Cardin and Courrèges, and various advertising techniques.

But to get back to the story, two big exhibitions in New York "Abstract Constructive Art from Malevich to tomorrow", in 1960, and "The Responsive Eye" in 1965 toured the United States and made a big contribution to our success.

But Paris is the essential meeting place for these artists from Germany, South America, Denmark, Israel, Italy, Japan, Switzerland and the United States. The Paris museums have realized this and these artists have shown their work at the National Museum of Modern Art and the Modern Art Museum of the City of Paris, which hold temporary exhibitions of new work as well as showing their permanent collections. Their work has also been shown at the National Centre of Contemporary Art (the C.N.A.C.), at 11 Rue Berryer, which holds exhibitions reflecting all the current movements in art." 　　　　D. R.

Further information :

The two Denise René galleries—on the Right Bank at 124 Rue La Boétie and on the Left Bank at 196 Boulevard Saint-Germain—permanently show work by artists including Vasarely, Agam, Arp, Cruz Diez, Sonia Delaunay, Demarco, Herbin, Mortensen, Soto, Schoffer.

Various contemporary art movements are represented in Paris museums and art galleries. Unknown young artists show their work at galleries such as: Yvon Lambert, 15 Rue de l'Échaudé; Lucien Durand, 19 Rue Mazarine; Daniel Templon, 30 Rue Beaubourg.

Pop and new realist art can be seen at: Mathias Fels, 138 Boulevard Haussmann (César, Dufrêne, Fontana, Yves Klein, Spoerri); Iris Clert, 3 Rue Duphot (Takis); and Alexandre Iolas, 196 Boulevard Saint-Germain (Yves Klein, Lalanne, Niki de Saint-Phalle, Tinguely). Iolas also specializes in Surrealist painting (Max Ernst, Magritte), as does André-François Petit, 122 Boulevard Haussmann (Bellmer, Brauner, Dali, Max Ernst, Tanguy) and, at the same address, Jacques Tronche (Max Ernst, Matta, Picabia). The Sonnabend gallery, at 12 Rue Mazarine, shows work by contemporary American artists.

Tachism, abstract expressionism and "raw art" can be seen at the Jeanne Bucher gallery, 53 Rue de Seine (Dubuffet, Tobey, Vieira da Silva), and at Jacques Dubourg, 126 Boulevard Haussmann (Lanskoy, Lapicque, Riopelle, Nicolas de Staël).

School of Paris art can be seen at the Galerie de France, 3 Rue du Faubourg-Saint-Honoré (Hartung, Manessier, Pignon, Singier, Soulages, Zao Wou Ki), while contemporary artists from a particularly wide range of movements show their work at the Claude Bernard gallery at 5 Rue des Beaux-Arts (Bacon, Balthus, Max Ernst, Kandinsky, Laurens, Picasso).

Among the galleries which show the great Cubist and abstract painters of this century are: Louise Leiris, 47 Rue de Monceau (Picasso, Braque, Giacometti, Juan Gris, Kandinsky, Léger, Miró), and Berggruen, 70 Rue de l'Université (Braque, Chagall, Klee, Matisse, Miró, Picasso).

The Maeght gallery, 13 Rue de Téhéran, has a big collection of contemporary abstract painting.

This only gives a glimpse of the immense range of artistic activity in Paris. Those who want further information should consult a monthly publication called the *Officiel des Galeries,* which costs 5 francs and is on sale at most newsstands and art bookshops.

For twenty-five years, Maurice Rheims was one of Paris's most distinguished auctioneers, and as such gained a particular insight into the psychology of collecting as well as the financial aspects of the art market. He has written several books, including important histories of Art Nouveau and nineteenth-century sculpture, each of which is marked by a fascination with the strange and the unusual. In 1972 Maurice Rheims retired to devote himself to writing.

Antiques

"Paris shares with London and New York the distinction of being one of the three great capitals of greatest interest to the curio-hunter.

In the 7th Arrondissement, for instance, it is easier to buy a Louis Quinze commode or a Greek statue than a loaf of bread. In fact there are about 1,000 antique shops in Paris, some of which stock objects which many a museum would be proud of.

If you look in the window of Alain Brieux's shop at 46 Rue Jacob, you are liable to find that its scholarly and amusing proprietor has displayed a seventeenth-century ivory skull next to a fœtus sleeping its everlasting sleep inside a glass flask blown in the Italian town of Murano.

Quai Voltaire and its neighbour Quai Malaquais are the Mecca of the antique-hunter in Paris. In the window of M. Carmontel's shop at 5 Quai Malaquais, you

may find a dish which once belonged to Frederick the Great... or you may find a ball of sulphur. It all depends on M. Carmontel's mood. On the corner, at 1 Rue des Saint-Pères, MM. Grognot and Joinel's wares reflect their owners' impeccable taste, while further down the street at number 11, Simone de Monbrison sells ancient statues from the Mediterranean and elsewhere.

Returning to Quai Voltaire, at number 5 M. Bresset offers fourteenth-century polychrome statues of St. Anne and St. George, and perhaps a 400-year-old dresser from the Loire region. For those whose passion is ceramics, I recommend a visit to 7 Quai Voltaire to meet M. Nicolier, who is a great expert on Italian majolica. Porcelain fanciers should go to 23 Quai Voltaire, where M. Vandermeersch rules urbanely over his kingdom of Saxe and Sèvres. Ten yards away at number 25, the mischievous and intelligent Huguette Bérès presides over a stock which includes Hokusai prints, Vuillards and Bonnards.

From Quai Voltaire we turn down Rue du Bac, stopping for a moment to see contemporary art enthusiast Daniel Gervis in his gallery at number 34, before turning left along Boulevard Saint-Germain as far as Jean-Michel Beurdeley's shop at number 200. A passionate connoisseur, M. Beurdeley is enormously gifted at displaying his Japanese and Chinese objects.

Jean Roudillon, whose gallery is at 198 Boulevard Saint-Germain, buys and sells a little of everything from primitive art to Art Nouveau, as the fancy takes him.

Meanwhile, on the other side of the river, at 48 Rue de Courcelles, the beautiful and competent Jeanine Loo officiates in a fantastic house built like a pagoda over a magnificent collection of treasures from the Orient.

No account of Paris antique dealers, however selective, could possibly omit Charles Ratton (14 Rue de Marignan), who loves his treasures so much that he can scarcely bring himself to sell them.

But there are many, many names I have not mentioned; great names like Wildenstein and Maeght, and Karl Flinker, who specializes in contemporary painting and whose gallery is in Rue de Tournon.

If I have left Knoll (268 Boulevard Saint-Germain) and Mobilier International (8 Rue des Saints-Pères) until last, it is because I was afraid that people might go to see them first, get interested in modern design, and then not bother to visit my friends the antique dealers and secondhand goods merchants who bring their own special touch of beauty to Paris." M. R.

Yves Saint-Laurent *was born in 1936 in Oran and grew up there. He worked with Christian Dior from 1953 until Dior's death in 1957, when he became artistic director of the house. His first collection had an enormous success with the trapeze line. In 1961 he decided to open his own fashion house, and since then he has branched out into accessories made and marketed under his name—scarves, ties, bags, jewellery, perfume, and so on—and, since 1966, the Saint-Laurent Rive Gauche shops.*

The haute couture

"The history of fashion, especially the history of the haute couture, is intimately bound up with the history of Paris. In fact Paris and the haute couture are almost synonymous.

Christian Dior died in 1957, Chanel and Balenciaga in 1971. But fashion is like the hydra—in spite of those who would like to slay it, the beast lives on and thrives as one of the last bastions of individuality.

The haute couture is a fragile business which must be preserved. It owes its existence to a tradition of fine workmanship, and its reputation is due as much to those who work in the background as to the talent of the couturiers themselves.

Today, however, because of adverse economic circumstances and the attractions of ready-to-wear, the haute couture sometimes seems to be losing ground. In reality, however, the difficulties it faces are reinforcing its prestige and authority. No question mark hangs over its future. For some it is a refuge; for others, a laboratory. It is one of the last bastions of craftsmanship. It draws its energy from the universal human need to escape from uniformity and to keep alive the possibility of creating a unique product.

The haute couture is not a myth. It is a reality. Through it and it alone, the traditions, the secrets of the craft are perpetuated. It alone is capable of achieving perfection of line, precision of cutting, the balanced design of a garment.

Fashion runs parallel to the haute couture, with which it should not be confused. It belongs to everyone. It is born anywhere and belongs to anyone who seeks it. But only the haute couture can give it sharpness and definition: it is to fashion what Molière and Racine are to the theatre."

Y. S.-L.

The son of a well-known collector, Valentine Abdy *is the head of Sotheby's and Parke-Bernet in Paris, where he has lived for seventeen years.*

Parisian by adoption

"Paris has a reputation of indifference towards the outside world and yet it is perhaps on account of this undeniable chauvinism that it has been able to conserve its essential character beyond the reach of outside influence.

There exists today, as there has always existed, a very broad-minded atmosphere which allows both the rich and the poor to meet each other on the same intellectual and social level. It is perhaps on account of this exchange of ideas, more noticeable here than elsewhere, that Paris is recognized as being the most civilized city in Europe.

What in English is called high society is known in France as the *beau monde* or literally the beautiful world. The women, without being more lovely, have each that purely female instinct which draws a profit from every little quality they may have to attract the opposite sex. Sometimes they even go to the point of underlining their own deficiencies, if only to separate themselves from the rest. Above all they benefit from this underlying sensibility which goes far further than mere coquetry and which has belonged to them for so many centuries.

The men have the reputation of being both cynical and difficult to approach, yet they are a part of the city and it is these same failings which keep intact the strange and inexplicable unity between them.

The longer one lives in Paris, the more one enjoys the discovery of its secrets, and one ends by being captivated by its reticence and by trembling at the idea that the city might suddenly reveal everything to those people who merely pass through without taking the trouble to understand all the things they see.

Known in the 18th century as "the city of light," its critics pretend that today everything is in darkness. Nevertheless, it is still in Paris that the most extravagant and extraordinary parties are given, and although they owe much to personal wealth, they owe even more to that tradition of refinement and æsthetic taste which is inherent in the French. Great balls are held in beautiful houses all over the world but, to cite only one example, the idea of leaving an enormous château in complete darkness with only a group of candles burning at every window—thereby leaving everything to the imagination—that idea is purely French and more precisely Parisian.

Finally, the nightclubs, the restaurants and the open-air cafés are so well known that visitors can easily initiate themselves into the city, providing that they never forget that like every other woman she keeps her heart well hidden."

V. A.

INDEX

154

PHOTOGRAPHS

The photos on the jacket are by Jacques Verroust (the Ile de la Cité) and Guy Le Querrec (the waiters of Brasserie Lipp).
Alecio de Andrade (Magnum): 27, 63 left / Dr Auhagen, Zefa (Rapho): 116 / Bruno Barbey (Magnum): 18, 26 left, 30 below left, 102 below / Albert Bazin (Fotogram): 79 / Pierre Belzeaux (Rapho): 76 / Pierre Bérenger: 66, 101 / Édouard Berne (Fotogram): 44 / Jean Biaugeaud: 145 right / Jean Bottin: 36, 40 below, 41, 43 below, 83, 84, 100 above, 123 right, 135 / Édouard Boubat (Top): 64 above / Maximilien Bruggmann: 130 right / Claude Caroly: 37 below, 38 above, 42, 59, 67, 93, 95, 120, 134 above / Henri Cartier-Bresson (Magnum) 21 / Jean-Philippe Charbonnier (Top): 25, 71, 97, 106 below / François Chauvaud (Fotogram): 110 below / Serge Chirol: 6 / Charles Ciccione (Rapho): 38 below, 49, 70, 74, 106 above, 117, 122, 134 below / J.-Ch. Crispoldi: 150 / Alain Dagbert (Viva): 26 right, 43 above, 128 / Danèse (Rapho): 51 / François Darras: 75 / Christian Dautreppe (Atlas Photo): 104 left / Yves Dejardin (Rapho): 107 above / Michel Desjardins (Top): 50, 152 left / Robert Doisneau (Rapho): 56 right, 90 left / Faillet (Ziolo): 64 below / Flammarion: 148 / Tibor Fulop (Fotogram): 14 / Marc Garanger: 17, 61 above, 133 / Olivier Garros (Top): 10, 11, 46, 80, 81, 90 right, 113 / Bernard Gérard (Fotogram): 94 / Giraudon: 144 right / Hervé Gloaguen (Viva): 139 / Louis Goldman (Rapho): 65 below / Roger Guillemot (Top): 48, 53, 89 / Jacques Guilloreau (Fotogram): 28 below / Jacqueline Guillot (Top): 15 / Ernst Haas (Magnum): 112 / Erich Hartmann (Magnum): 108 /

Francisco Hidalgo: 7, 31 above right, 99, 129 / Dominique Lecouvette: 144 / Jean-Pierre Leloir (Association du Paris historique): 57 / Charles Lénars: 92, 130 right / Gérard Loucel (Fotogram): 37 above / Magnum: 115 / Marie-Claire: 153 / Guy Marineau (Top): 20 / Pierre-Louis Millet (Top): 82 / Inge Morath (Magnum): 119 / Jean Mounicq (Fotogram): 13 / Michel Nahmias: 22, 24, 30 above left, 47 above, 52 right, 56 left, 103, 114, 123 left, 127 / Janine Niepce (Rapho): 28 above, 40 left, 78 above / William Oswen: 96 / Jacques Pavlovsky (Rapho): 98, 141 / Alain Perceval: 45, 91 / Phédon Salou: 105 / Paul Pougnet (Rapho): 110 above / Jean-Noël Reichel: 8, 54, 55, 118 / Marc Riboud (Magnum): 104 right / René Roland (Ziolo): 39, 60 / André Sas (Rapho): 136 / Serge de Sazo (Rapho): 140 / Michel Serraillier (Rapho): 126 / Jean-Loup Sieff: 152 right / Top: 102 above, 149 / Georges Tourdjmann (Top): 32, 33 / Eddy Van der Veen (Rapho): 58, 100 below / Jacques Verroust: 9, 12, 16, 19, 23, 29, 31 below right, 34, 35, 47 below, 52 below left, 61 below, 62, 63 right, 65 above, 68, 69, 72, 73, 77, 78 below, 85, 86, 87, 107 below, 109, 111, 121, 124, 125, 131, 132, 137, 138 145 below left.
Map of Lutetia, by Nicolas de Fer (p. 144): Bibliothèque historique de la Ville de Paris.
The Palace and the Sainte-Chapelle, from "The Very Rich Hours of the Duc de Berry" (p. 144): Musée Condé, Chantilly.
© SPADEM 1973: 59 (Maillol, *The River*), 64 (Renoir, *Le Moulin de la Galette*), 66 (Monet, *Les Nymphéas*), 80-81 (Rodin, *The Kiss* and *The Gate of Hell*).
© ADAGP 1973: 106 (Chagall, the ceiling at the Opéra).
The map showing the development of Paris (p. 145) and the plan of the Louvre (p. 147) are taken from the *Guide Bleu PARIS* (1972 edition, Librairie Hachette).